The Unheard Predicament

Social and Legal Perspective on Women and Child Rights

The Unheard Predicament

Social and Legal Perspective on Women and Child Rights

Aishwarya Chaturvedi

KALPAZ

ISBN: 978-93-5128-239-6

Price: ₹ 190

First Published, 2017

Published by

Kalpaz Publications
C-30, Satyawati Nagar,
Delhi – 110052
E-mail: kalpaz@hotmail.com
Ph.: 9212142040

Printed at: G. Print Process, Delhi

Cataloging in Publication Data—DK
Courtesy: D.K. Agencies (P) Ltd. <docinfo@dkagencies.com>

Chaturvedi, Aishwarya, author.
The unheard predicament : social & legal perspective on women & child rights / Aishwarya Chaturvedi.
pages cm
Includes bibliographical references.
ISBN 9789351282396

1. Women's rights—India. 2. Children's rights—India. 3. Women's rights—Social aspects—India. 4. Children's rights—Social aspects—India. I. Title.

KNS516.C43 2016 DDC 342.540878 23

Contents

Part – II

Preface

The Unheard Predicament is a series of reflections on the questions that have haunted the mind of every Indian and perhaps, every person in the world. The possibility of equal rights and status to every individual, women and children in particular, is the underlying theme in all the essays in this book. As we grow up, equality is something that one yearns for. However, the realisation of the fundamental inequity comes by looking around and through experience. The fact that equal rights and opportunities is not a reality around us while inequality is, comes as a disorienting experience, which makes keeping a balance amidst overwhelming circumstances naturally difficult. The Unheard Predicament, is an attempt to ask and at times formulate answers to questions such as:

"Do we live in an equal society?"

"Are all of us accorded equal rights and status in a society?"

"If yes, then do all of us get to enjoy such rights?"

"Has our society successfully done away with gender roles?"

"Do women and children get to exercise their due rights?"

The Unheard Predicament deals with the said questions from a legal, philosophical and sociological perspective.

There are two main indicators pointed out by Dr Amartya Sen. The educational inequality and health inequality are the indicators of the status of a woman welfare. In India, irrespective of caste, creed or religion, the status of women is lower than that of men. Gender-based discrimination against females, is unfortunately pervasive all across the world. Some argue that such discrimination or inferior treatment results in the failure of females to understand their rights. This is predominant in India as well as in other lesser developed nations such as Pakistan, Bangladesh, Afghanistan, South Korea and the like. However, there has been a universal consensus on the need for gender equality. It is a subject of great concern and even greater social significance.

Part A of the book begins with explaining the need for women rights and the current status of females in the society. It further, elaborates on the various sources of law that are prevalent and also the vital theory of John Austin's concept of positive laws. Thereafter, the next chapter discusses the concept of society and the two predicaments namely, socio-centric and atman-centric, as formulated by Professor Daya Krishna.

The subsequent chapter discuss the rights accorded to females by our Constitution and the lacunaes present in their implementation. It also includes data of crimes, social evils such as child marriage, dowry etc., violence in the form of rape, domestic violence, acid attacks, sexual harassment at workplace and the like, committed against women in India. Further, this book lays down the concept of negative and positive freedom and liberty as conceptualised by Sir Isaiah Berlin.

Part A concludes by suggesting exhilaration of women in the society by formulating remedies such as facilitating quality education and jobs to females, providing them with a vehicle to commute, hence making them independent in some sense and it also suggests setting up of few redressal mechanisms along with other things.

Part B of the book talks about child rights conferred upon children in India by our Constitution and also by international legislations such as the UNCRC and initiatives like UNICEF. It further raises the important question as to whether all children get these rights? The answer is in the non-affirmative. There are various lacunaes in the implementation of such rights.

The next chapter, discusses the rights and remedies available to children such as right to education, schemes like one laptop per child, prohibition of child labour, child trafficking, begging, child marriages, right to be heard, right to healthcare and nutrition, etc. It also brings to light the importance of education and the dismal face of our society in providing such education to the scheduled castes and scheduled tribes of our country, who are vital for the progress of the nation.

The subsequent chapters deal with social and philosophical aspects which contribute in formulating laws, such as the concepts of customary and reflective morality. Thereafter, Kant's notion of categorical imperatives are discussed which put forth the point that a right or an act should be independent of the good. Kant's theory was anti-consequentialist and deontological ethics.

Further, this book elaborates on the juvenile justice system in India and the various problems associated with treating juveniles as adults. The theory of capital punishment is also discussed at length to bring out the cons of treating them as adults.

Finally, Part B concludes with discussing what according to Aristotle is the highest moral ideal. His ethics is teleological and suggests every man to adopt a middle path in life and avoid the extremes. This helps in understanding the theory of reforming and understanding juvenile offenders.

The Unheard Predicament aims to evoke a thought amongst its readers that in today's times it is imperative that women and children, being two of the major development indicators, get their due rights and an equal status in the society. The law indeed facilitates such rights and justice, but even we, as common people can individually work towards ensuring such justice and fairness to our fellow beings and aid our administration in successful implementation of laws. This would help us march towards a better future and contribute in the progress of our nation as a whole.

Acknowledgements

A great many people have contributed in making this book possible. To begin with, I would like to thank my teachers who have taken the effort to give shape to my ideas. This book is nothing but reflections on the knowledge handed down by some of the distinguished minds in the Indian academia and their influence on the thought of a student. These teachers include Dr Devasia M Antony, Dr Rekha Basu, Mr Sumit Nandan, Dr Kamala Sankaran, Ms Anju Sinha, Mr Parikshet Sirohi and mentors (Hon'ble Justice Mr Ashok Bhushan, Hon'ble Chief Justice G. Rohini, Delhi High Court; Senior Advocate Mr Siddharth Luthra, Mr Viraj Gandhi, Mr Sameer Chaudhary, Ms Shraddha Karol, Mrs Mayuri Raghuvanshi, Ms Anureeta Sharma) who helped me see the practical side of things allowed me opportunities to work for worthy causes that lent insight as well as experience in putting thoughts to practice. Also, I would like to thank my family members (Late Sh. Sushil Chandra Chaturvedi, Sh Ashoke Chaturvedi, Smt Rajini Chaturvedi, Dr Apurv Chaturvedi, Smt. Archana Chaturvedi, Sh. Atul Chaturvedi, Smt. Rachna Chaturvedi, Sh. Abhinav Chaturvedi, Smt Neeta Chaturvedi, Smt. Swapna Chaturvedi, Mr Sandeep Chaturvedi, Mr Sushant Chaturvedi, Ms Eesha Chaturvedi, Mr Eeshan Chaturvedi, Mr Lokmanyu Chaturvedi, Ms Divya Chaturvedi, Mr Abhisht Chaturvedi and Mr Prateek Singh) who always extended support and encouragement to my endeavours even if they did not seem rational every time. Most importantly, I would like to thank my elder brother Mr Arpit Chaturvedi for giving me the impetous to author this book and for always guiding me in every walk of life. Further, I would like to thank my friends (Ms Upasana Singh, Ms Ishika Chawla, Ms Vijaya Chhaparia, Mr Anuj Arora, Ms Sakshi Kalra, Ms Meghna Dabur, Ms Sheena Aggarwal, Mr Kartikey Raj Gupta, Mr Balbhadra Singh, Ms Vrinda Rajvanshi, Ms Ashna Mehta, Ms Shreya Jain,

Ms Dhanvi Shree Telang, Ms Kavya Bhatnagar, Ms Ruchi Gupta and many others) who helped me in various ways ranging from discussing ideas over long walks, challenging my view points, and going through my work umpteen times to suggest improvements. Finally, a credit to libraries is due (Hindu College Library, Campus Law Centre, Faculty of Law University of Delhi Library and Human Resource Development Library) for their invaluable inputs.

Part – I

Women Rights

Women rights are not a mere necessity but are imperative for the society. Well, at least for a civilised one. However, the question of according special rights to women, has been received rather preposterously by majority of our society, more often than not. People who are against according special rights to women always put forth this age old question that 'men and women are equal' and if they are equal then why accord special rights only to women? Then what follows is a metaphorical affray on a colossal level.

In order to avoid this affray, we need to ask ourselves a fundamental question as to are men and women really equal? If I were to answer this question, I would answer in the negative. According to me, men and women are not equal. God created them differently; physically, biologically, psychologically. When God did not intend us to be equal, then how could we assert such egalitarianism to our beings? However, the only and perhaps, the most important aspect in which God did intend us to be equal is for all of us to have a right to life and dignity. Everybody has a right to dignity which they should not be denied.

It's a well known fact that ours is a patriarchal society. Hence, women have been subservient to men, socially. However, there are parts of the world (like, India) where matriarchy is prevalent and therefore, men play the subordinate role. The Naga community residing in the north-eastern region of India and some tribes in Africa are examples of a matriarchal society. So, how can we say that men and women are equal? It sometimes makes me wonder in jest if there were an actual relation between development of nations and patriarchy! As the great scholar, Mr P. Sainath had once rightly said, "they (females in India) have subsumed their suppression in such fashion that they are not even aware whether their rights are being taken away from them or not, still they are leading happy lives. The realisation of suppression has been wiped of, what else can we expect now!"

In order to place them equally on the social pedestrian, we need to accord special rights to that gender which lags behind the other. In our society that gender would be female. The very mind-set of one sex being superior to the other, needs to change. When every human being has been accorded the right to life and liberty by our Constitution, then how can one sex be subservient to the other?

"In the last three decades, the women's movements have increasingly sought to influence state policy with a view to include women issues and perspectives and increase women's representation and participation. As a result of this activism and gradual transformation sparked by the women's movement, governments in various countries, especially in the third world took steps to reform existing laws, incorporated policy directives on women and development in the planning process and initiated women specific programmes and projects. Since the mid-seventies, there has also been global debate to eliminate women's inequality through effective mechanisms that could implement the new commitment to women's equality and participation and monitor its results. In India, the establishment of Women's Welfare and Development Bureau and a National Plan of Action in 1976 followed the Report of the Committee on the Status of Women in India. The recommendations of the World Plan of Action for the International Women's Decade had also included the creation of such national agencies. As a result, cells, bureaus, departments or ministries to look after the interests of women started becoming a significant part of governmental structures in the late 1970s. The experience of women's groups with such and other state agencies have led to the debate as to whether or to what extent these new forms of organisations have been able to carry forward the feminist agenda of women's movements and also have been able to incorporate practices consistent with feminist values of broad participation in those arenas. If women still continue to be peripheral to the planning and the political process, it means that such machineries have not succeeded in the objective of mainstreaming or integrating women in development. In India, too, as the national machinery evolved and as India was responding to the demands of women's movements and initiatives of UN, the debates within and outside the movement continued on as to what kind of mechanisms would yield best results. Overtime an assessment of mechanisms so created has mostly been negative, as it has come out from a critical examination of the nature of government response to questions of gender, structures, agencies and programmes, action plans and state policies and state initiatives that has been done with a view to understand whether there have been gaps in conceptualising gender issues within governance, or there are problems at the implementation level or there are not enough spaces available to women to influence policy and processes for bringing required changes. The policy documents of the State have incorporated the rhetoric of gender progressive perspectives and the documents most freely use the vocabulary of 'empowerment', equity, development, justice, and rights of women, increasing the capabilities and participation of women etc. without any comparable change in the position of women in Indian society. And while there have been some efforts to amend laws with a view to make them gender just, the changes have not been requisite. At the policy-making level too, improving women's rights in property and their access to other productive resources has not become a priority issue. By 1970s, as more and more evidence with regard to the subordinate status and position started coming in and women's issues were vociferously raised by women's movements all over the world, it was also emphasised that the state has to take the responsibility and lead in achieving the objective of gender equality by incorporating women's perspectives and concerns in its policies and structures. In 1971, on a request from United Nations to prepare a report on women's status, the Government of India (GOI) constituted a national level Committee to review the status of women in India since independence. The Department of Social Welfare was identified to do this. Phulrenu Guha, the then minister-in-charge of Social Welfare who was given this responsibility insisted that such a study about women's status in Indian society should be considered a national imperative since, while reviews had been undertaken of the condition and status of Scheduled Castes and Backward Classes, there has not been a similar kind of study on women.

She even proposed constitution of a Commission of Enquiry for the purpose.

The Committee on the Status of Women in India, whose report coincided with the International Women's Year, compiled evidence of gender gaps in virtually every sector and highlighted the inequalities suffered by women in the spheres of employment, health and education and the failure of government to ensure the application of rights guaranteed by the Constitution to women. The Committee pointed out that the Indian State has failed in its constitutional responsibility of not discriminating on grounds of gender. On a stronger note it said that there seemed to be no acknowledgement of women's work and needs in all the major sectors of Indian economy. In fact, women had been increasingly viewed by the planners as not being in need of an independent livelihood, to the point where women's decreasing work participation rate and share of employment increasing poverty and insecurity in sectors of the economy in which they used to dominate earlier (forestry, agriculture, livestock, cottage industry, sericulture, fisheries etc.) were not even viewed as problems requiring change".[1]

Article 14 of our Constitution also calls for unequal treatment in case of unequals and bars equal treatment in case of unequals. This unequal treatment is not to give any special or privileged treatment to one class of citizens over others, but to bring them at par with the other class of citizens.

Gandhi was partially correct when he referred to modern civilisation as "the satanic civilisation" because, India as a nation may have progressed technologically, economically and even socially in some pockets, but we still have a great distance to travel in order to be accorded the rubric of a socially and culturally advanced nation.

Of course, one cannot deny the fact that a lot of myths have been broken and many rudimentary beliefs have been done away with. Women in India today, experience certain freedom which was probably a far-fetched dream for them, many years ago. However, the darker side to this celebrated metamorphosis is that such freedom and dignity is experienced by only a negligible section of the society. Most of the women in our country are still being treated as animals.

Female foeticide and infanticide are still being practised in many parts of the country like Rajasthan and Haryana. The irony being that according to science, women have a biological advantage over men for long life and survival.

The much celebrated childhood of a girl child is still being transformed into the "celebrations" of her marriage in the form of child marriage and a girl, whether modern or conservative, is still being made to pay the price of exercising her freedom in the form of rape. This reminds me of a very peculiar incident of my childhood, which I still remember very vividly. We had gone to Mussoorie for our summer vacations. There is a place called 'Kempty Falls' on the outskirts of the city, its at a quite high altitude. There one could get dressed up as locals of the hills and get clicked. I got dressed in the local attire and was waiting for my turn to get clicked. I somehow lost my balance and was almost about to fall off the cliff when my father saved me just in time! Photographer standing there, after witnessing the entire event, uttered derisively to my father, 'kya sahib, ladki hi to hai! Mar bhi jaati to kya hota!' He was obviously shunned by my father in response to his statement. I was only eleven years old back then. His words shocked me! At that tender age itself, I had deciphered that a great deal was wrong with the mentality of our people and not all of us were living in the happy, developing India that was painted before us in our schools, after all.

In order to overcome the aforementioned evils of the society and many more, women need to be accorded special rights. More importantly, these rights must be put to effective use.

1

The Sources of Law[2]

A source of law means either the manufacture or origin of a law or the ability to impart a rule or norm the quality of law.

A source of law is any fact which in accordance with the law determines the judicial recognition and acceptance of any new rule as having the force of law.

Salmond classified the sources of law into two categories:

(a) *Legal or formal sources*:- These are those sources which are recognised as such by the law itself and are authoritative. From these sources a rule of law derives its force and validity. Examples, Constitution, statutes, precedents and customs recognised by the law.

(b) *Historical or material sources*:- These are the sources which are lacking recognition by the law and are unauthoritative. The historical sources are sources in fact only. From these sources, a rule of law derives the matter but not the validity. Examples, legal writings, juristic opinions or even foreign constitutions, statutes, etc.

The decision of the court is a legal source while the ultimate materials on which it is based are historical sources.

Sources of law differ from system to system and society to society. Since in India, we have common law system, Constitution, legislatives precedents and customs are our legal sources of law. In some matter, personal law (ran, smirities, etc.) is also a source of law:

1. **Constitution:** Constitution differs from legislation in so far as legislation finds its authority in the Constitution while the

Constitution is the ultimate source and its authority lies in the political fact that it has been so accepted. The source of all rights and legislation in India is Constitution which enshrines within itself the Directive Principles of State Policy and the Fundamental Rights. Our Constitution is the Fundamental law of the country. Its provisions lay down binding rules, violation of which can be check and remedied through court action.

2. **Customs:** Custom is the oldest and most important source of law. In the evolution of the human society, it appears to be beyond doubt that custom arose first law came later. Law was built upon custom Law denotes a more definitive organisation of human society with some kind of power structure established (viz. State).

According to Salmond, "Custom is to society what law is to the state."

Dr Allen defines custom as the uniformity of habits or conduct of people under like circumstances. When people find any act to be good and beneficial, apt and agreeable to their nature and disposition they used and practice it from time to time, and it is by frequent use and multiplication of this act that the custom is made."

Customs arise whenever a few human beings come together, as no association, of human beings can exist permanently without adopting consciously or unconsciously, some definite rules governing reciprocal rights and obligation. The growth of a custom, however, is not the result of conscious thought but of tentative practices.

Usage developing into customary law is the oldest form of law-making and in its early stages depends for its validity on the willingness of those who generally follow the usage to submit to it. According to Oxford Dictionary, custom means, established usage having the force of law.

Kinds of customs: All customs which have the force of law are of two kinds:

(a) Conventional custom

(b) Legal custom

A **conventional custom** is a established practice which is legally binding not because of any legal sanction, but because it has been expressly or impliedly incorporated in a contract between the parties concerned.

Legal customs may be special or general, former may include a families customs amongst the members of a particular tribe, a local custom obtaining in a particular locality general custom on the other hand, times all the persons within a community, it consists of the law that has been declared and created by the reported decisions of the superior courts of justice.

Legal Customs	*Conventional Customs*
1. To be valid, must be supported by immemorial antiquity	Does not require any antiquity
2. Does not normally conflict with the statute.	May face such conflict

Western Jurists View of Custom

Custom is regarded as a source of law the Western jurists, though they assign importance to it to a varying degree depending upon their approach and outlook.

Analytical Jurists- Austin having defined law as the command of a political superior or definite human authority addressed to political inferiors and enforced by penalty or sanction, held that custom becomes a law only when it receives judicial or legislative recognition. Customarily law is no law at all or it is imperfect or inchoate law.

Allen disagrees with Austins thesis. He regards custom as "self-contained, self-sufficient, and self-justified law: and says that the function of the court is "declaratory rather than constitutive.

The Analytical theory, does not very much fit the Indian condition. As in India, long before the advert of the British, customs were observed by the people and were enforced not by the courts but by the village or community panchayats.

Historical Jurists-They attached a much greater importance to custom. They held that all early law was customary and that the function of legislation is limited to supplementing and redefining custom. According to Saving, the real bases of all positive law are to be found in the general consciousness of people (Volksgeist). The source of law is that the command of the sovereign, not even the habits of a community, but the instinctive sense of right possessed by every race However, not all customs are consciously created growth of much customarily law is the result of tentative practice.

Hindu and Muslim View of Customs

Customs have always been given a very important place as a source of law by the Hindu Jurists. Two views have prevailed regarding the relative value of customs vis-à-vis the sruti and smriti. The Dharmashastra writers subordinated customs to sruti and smriti which were given a higher authority. Thus, according to Gautam, Dharmas (customs) of countries, castes and families, which are not opposed to vedic scriptures, are authoritative and binding. Mitakshara, Dayabhag, Mayukha also place custom as subordinate to sruti and smriti.

Some of the smritis underlined the significance of customs by saying that suppression of customs would give rise to resentment and rebellion. In one text of the Manusmriti itself, there is a hint to regard custom as superior to everything.

The Hindu Jurists were liberal in their them (customs) e.g. the eight forms of marriage were recognised by Dharmashtra writers even though some of the forms were highly objectionable.

Muslim view of custom- The two principal sources of the Islamic law are the Quran as containing the word of God and the hadis or traditions, being the inspired utterances of the Prophet and precedents derived from his acts. Next important sources are: *izma*, the consensus of opinion amongst the learned; *urf* or custom; and *qiyas*, the analogical deductions from the first three. In Quran there is not much of law. There is no doubt that, during his life time, the Prophet himself recognised the force of customary law.

The conditions laid down for the validity of custom, under the Muslim law are:

(1) It must be generally prevalent in the country.

(2) It must not be merely a local usage in a village or a town, though it need not be ancient or immermorial.

(3) It must be an established course of conduct, not merely a practice on a afew occasions.

(4) Custom being essentially territorial, it cannot affect the law in other lands, as it is confined to a particular period it cannot affect the custom in another age.

Essentials of a valid custom:

(1) Reasonableness

(2) Consistency

(3) Compulsory observance

(4) Continuity and Immemorial Antiquity

(5) Certainly

— Custom in the Indian legal system

— Proof of a accustom

— Abrogation of custom

(3) Legislation- These are two obvious reasons for legislation being regarded as one of the most effective sources of law:

(i) It involves lying down of legal rules by the legislature which the State recognises as law.

(ii) It has the force and authority of the State.

Legislation means 'making of law'. It is that source of law which consists in the declaration of legal rules by a competent authority, e.g. Parliament or State legislatures. According to Bentham and John Stuart Mill, legislation includes both, the process of law making and the law evolved as a result of this process.

Legislation may be of Two Kinds-

Supreme and Subordinate Legislation.

When the Sovereign authority itself makes the law, it is supreme legislation. Subordinate or delegated legislation is by and other authority than the sovereign by virtue of powers delegated to it by the sovereign, and subject to the control of sovereign.

In our legal system, Acts of Parliament and the ordinances and other laws made by the President and Governors, are supreme legislation and includes rules, regulations, by laws, orders, directions, notifications, etc. made by various authorities such as corporations, municipalities, universities, government department, Supreme is High Courts etc. The Supreme legislation is not superior to the constitution and it is subject to various constitutional limitations e.g. a legislation which infringes the fundamental rights of citizens is invalid. Further, Supreme legislation cannot delegate the "essential" legislative functions which relate to the making of policy.

(1) Certainty and precision

(2) Instrument of legal form

(3) Conforms to natural justice

Legislation vs. Customs

(1) The existence of legislation is essentially *dejure* whereas customary law exists *de facto*.

(2) The authority of legislation lies in the express will of the state. Customs are general based on the will of the people and have only implied authority of the state.

(3) Legislation grows out of the theoretical principles but customary law grows out of practice and long existence.

(4) Legislation is complete, precise and written whereas customary law is mostly unwritten.

(5) **Precedent-** The term "precedent" refers to a previous instance or case which is or may be taken as an example or rule for subsequent cases or by which some similar acts or circumstances may be supported or justified (Oxford Dictionary). In short, it means the employment of past decisions as guides in the moulding of future decisions Salmond defines precedent as the making of law by the recognition and application of new rules by the court themselves in the administration of justice. The doctrine of

precedent provides the evidence of what the law is on a particular time precedent become binding depends on the main factors namely-

(i) it must have been pronounced by a law which is sufficiently senior; and

(ii) it is only the ratio decidendi i.e. reasoning behind the decision which is binding.

Blackstone pointed out that it is an established rule to abide by the former precedents where the same points come again in litigation.

Justice Cordage also supports the view that adherence to precedent should be the rule and not an exception.

Kinds of precedents- Precedents may either be authoritative or persuasive. An authoritative precedent is one which has a binding force and the Judge must follow it whether he approves it or not. These are the decisions of superior court of justice which are binding on subordinate courts.

Persuasive precedent (historical source) on the other hand is one which the Judges are under no obligation to follow but which the maybe taken into consideration. The decision of the Supreme Court of India is and authoritative precedent for all courts in India but for the Supreme Court itself, it has only persuasive value. Similar is the case with High Court.

Circumstances which destroy the binding force of Judicial precedents:-

(1) Ignorance of statute

(2) Inconsistency between earlier decision of higher court

(3) Erroneous decisions

(4) Precedent sub silentio

(5) Affirmation or reversal on different ground

Do Judges Make Law?

It is a debatable question as to whether judges make law or simply declare an existing one. According to the declaratory theory of precedent, the Judges, do not make law they merely declare it, that is to say when a cause overrules a decision, it does not performs a new rule, but only declares that the suppose a law was never law. Even Blackstone has accepted this view. He observed that the function of the judge is to discover in the existing law the principles that govern the facts of individual cases. Thus, judges maintaining and explain the existing law, hence they are law-finders and not law-makers. Austin calls declaratory theory as hypocritical and a childish fiction employed by common law judges that law is not made by them.

True, the primary function of a Judge is to adjudicate the conflicting claims and not to lay down a new law, but he cannot refuse to decide a case on the ground that the law is silent or obscure on the point. In such a (new) situation the judge not only decides but also applies and lays down an entirely new legal rule.

In India, the Supreme Court overruled the ***Golaknath***[3] decision in the historic Fundamental Rights case, namely ***Keshwananda Bharti vs State of Kerala***[4] and laid down a new basic structures theory. In this case the court held that the parliament can alter any provision of the constitution except the basic structure of the constitution.

Legislation vs. Precedent

(1) The legislation has its source in the law-making will of the state whereas precedent has its source in judicial decisions.

(2) Legislation is generally prospective whereas precedent is retrospective in nature.

(3) Legislation is declared or published before it is brought into force but precedent comes into force at once i.e. as soon as decision is pronounced.

(4) Legislation involves law-making by deductive method whereas case-law is created by resort to inductive method.

Merits and Demerits of Precedents

Merits

(1) Keeps up with the needs of the society.

(2) Practical.

(3) Certain and easy to understand.

(4) Provide useful guidelines to the Judges.

(5) Flexible.

Demerits

(1) Difficult to find a particular case.

(2) Arbitrary in character.

(3) Not certain.

(4) Erroneous decisions.

(5) Law must be known before it is enforced.

References: This chapter has been taken from the book *STUDIES IN JURISPRUDENCE & LEGAL THEORIES,* 7th Edition, by N.V. Paranjape.

2

John Austin's Concept of Positive Laws[5]

Generally speaking, legal positivism is the apposite of natural law. Legal positivism proposes that there isn't necessarily a connection between law and morality. Instead, it holds that law comes from various sources, usually the government. Under legal positivism there is no valid argument for breaking a law, even it the law isn't considered to be fair or fuse. Positive approach to law concentrates on things as they are not as they ought to be. The main concern of the positivists is law that is actually found, positum, and not the ideal law. The analytical school is positive in its approach to the legal problems in the society. John Austin is one of the main proponents of this school.

John Austin (1790-1859) is considered to be the father of English Jurisprudence. His lectures were published under the title *'The Province of Jurisprudence Determined.'* He confined his study only to the positive law and applied analytical method for this purpose. By positive law, Austin meant laws properly so called as distinguished from moral and other laws which he described as laws improperly so called which lack force or sanction of the state Austin described positive law as the aggregate of rule set by man as politically superior to men as politically inferior subject. He attributes (1) Command, (2) Sanction, (3) Duty, (4) Sovereignty as the four essential attribute of positive law.

Austin defined law as a rule laid down for the guidance of an intelligent being by an intelligent being having power over him, so called proper law includes: Law of God, Human Laws and Positive

Laws. The law improperly so called includes: Laws by analogy and Laws by metaphor. According to him, "positive morality" consists of: Law not set by men (as political superior) or in pursuance of fashion. The improper laws lacked sanction of the state. According to Justice Holmes, Austin's distinction between positive law and positive morality seeks to exclude the consideration of goodness or badness in the realm of law. In Austin positive law there is no place for idea or justness in law.

Law as a command: Positive Law, according to him, consists of commands, set as rules of conduct, by a sovereign member or member of the independent political society who the author of law is supreme. According to him, law is the command of a sovereign requiring his subjects to do or for bear from doing certain acts. There is an implied threat of a sanction if the command is not obeyed.

A command is an expressing of a wish by a determinate person, or body of persons that another person shall do or forbear from, doing some act subject to an evil in the event of disobedience. The evil which will probably be incurred in case, a command is disobeyed is called a 'sanction'. So every law is a command, imposing a duty, enforced by a sanction. It is only by the chance of incurring evil, that one is obliged to compliance.

According to him, a command maybe particular or occasional (addressed to one person or group of persons) or general (addressed to the community at large, they are also continuing commands).

The method German legal philosopher Gustav Radbreech also criticised Austinian conception of law, which in his opinion, leads to dictatorship as was the case in Germany during the Nazi rule.

Judicial commands are commonly occasional or particular, although the commands which they are calculated to enforce are commonly laws or rules.

Distinction between Law and Occasional Commands

(i) Commands which oblige generally the members of given community (or persons of given classes) are not always laws or rules – Where the Sovereign issues an order, enforced by penalties for a general mourning on occasion of a public calamity; the order obliges generally the members of entire community but it is not law or rule because it obliges to acts which it assign specifically.

(ii) Command which obliges exclusively persons individually determined, may amount to a law or rule, for example, a father may set a rule to his child. Certain of God's laws were as binding on the first man, as they are binding at this hour on the millions.

Most of the laws established by political superiors are general in a two-fold manner as enjoining or forbidding generally acts of kinds or sorts; and as binding the whole community. Thus, a law may be defined as a command which obliges a person/person to a course of conduct.

Imperative Theory of Law

Austin, however accepts that there are three kinds of laws which, though not commands, may be included within the perview of law by way of exception. They are as follows:-

(1) Declaratory or explanatory laws-These are not commands because they are already in existence and are passed only to explain the law which is already in force legislative interpretation (like judicial interpretation) establish new laws under the guise of explaining the old.

(2) Laws of repeal-Austin does not treat such laws as commands because they are in fact the revocation of a command. They release from duties imposed by existing laws, and named permissive laws or permissions such laws are often imperative.

(3) Laws of imperfect obligation-They are not treated as command because there is no sanction attached to them. Austin holds that command to become law, must be accompanied by duty and sanction for its enforcement. While an imperfect obligation also pertains to a religious or moral obligation (duty imposed by positive morality).

Criticism of Austin's Imperative/Command Theory of Law

Austinian theory of law and analytical positivism has been criticised by jurists like Bryce, Olivecrona and others. It has been criticised on the following grounds:-

(1) Idea of command inapplicable in modern society.

(2) Customs overlooked.

(3) Permissive character of law ignored.

(4) No place for Judge made law.

(5) Austins theory treats International law as mere morality.

(6) Command overemphasised.

(7) Inter-relationship between law and morality completely ignored.

(8) Sanction alone is not the means to induce obedience.

Concept of Sovereignty

The great contrast between positive law and positive morality was, in Austin's view, the fact that the former was set by a political superior. He elaborated this motion and evolved his theory of sovereignty, and the independent political society which sovereignty implies, is distinguished from other superiority or might and from other society, by the following marks or characters. Sovereignty involved two "marks" a positive and a negative one. The positive marks was that the bulk of a given society was in the habit of obedience to a determinate superior was not in the common superior. The negative mark was that the determinate superior was not in the habit of obedience to some other superior.

Austin's notion of sovereign is if a determinate human superior not in a habit of obedience to a like superior, receives habitual obedience from the bulk of a given society, that determinate superior is sovereign in that society. The basis of sovereignty is thus the face of obedience. The sovereign's power is unlimited and indivisible (no division of authority). The sovereign is not bound by any legal limitation or by his own laws. According to him, Constitutional law derives its force from the public opinion regarding its expediency and morality.

To show that union of those two marks renders a given society a society political and independent:-

(i) When obedience is rare or transient and not habitual or permanent, the relation of sovereignty and subjection is not created thereby.

(ii) Unless habitual obedience be rendered by bulk of society to one and the same superior, the given society is either in a state of nature of anarchy or is split into two or more independent political societies.

(iii) When that certain superior habitually obeys the command of a certain person or body, the society is not independent, although it may be political.

Criticism of Austenian Sovereignty

(1) According to Dias, sovereignty cannot be defined in terms of obedience. It cannot be said that sovereignty of the crown in parliament was established by the habitual obedience of the judges that established the sovereignty of the crown in parliament.

(2) The attribute of indivisibility has also created difficulty the question is whether sovereign authority can be vested in more than one body, not whether it may be exercised by more than one. Austinian theory could be applied to the British Parliament which is supreme (there is no division of power in England into different organs of the state). However, Austin's notion that sovereignty is individual is falsified by federal constitutions e.g. India.

(3) The attribute of continuity of the sovereign may be questioned by asking where sovereignty resides during dissolution of parliament. In one place, Austin said correctly that the sovereign body is the crown, the lords and the commons: but elsewhere he asserted that it is the crown, the lord and the Electorate. The latter interpretation renders the whole of his conception meaningless. Who, in that case the commander and who the commanded?

(4) Law before state-It is not necessary for the law to exist if the sovereign exists. There were societies prior to existence, of sovereign and there were rules that were in prevalence. At that point of time, there was no political superior. Law had its origin in custom, religion and public opinion. All these so called laws were later enforced by the political superior.

(5) International law-According to Austin international law lacks sanctions because there is no sovereign, hence no command which is to be obeyed by the state in mutual dealings. But in the present day context, nobody will accept that international law is not law (even if it lacks sanction).

Conclusion

Critics of Austin say that a theory of defining law in terms of command, sovereignty and sanctions alone cannot provide an adequate analysis of the ordinary standard type of legal system. Austins' insistence on sanctions as a mark of law conceals and distorts the real character and function of law in community.

Further, customs and conventions of the constitution though not enforceable by law, regulate the conduct of the people and the state. Austin's theory completely ignored customs which constitute very important part of any legal system. In *Raj Kapoor* vs. *State* (1980), Justice Krishna Iyer held "Jurisprudentially speaking, law in the sense of command to do or not to do, must be a reflection of the communities cultural norms not the state's regimentation of aesthetic expression or artistic creation."

In modern times, law is nothing but the general will of the people, therefore law cannot be said to be a mere command of the sovereign. Austin's theory was later improved upon by Holland, Salmond and Gray.

References: This chapter has been taken from the book *STUDIES IN JURISPRUDENCE & LEGAL THEORIES,* 7th Edition, by N.V. Paranjape.

3

The Two Predicaments and Notion of Freedom

Professor Daya Krishan's book, *Social Philosophy: Past and Future* was first published in 1969 on the basis of lecture delivered by him at the Indian Institute of Advanced Study in 1968. These lectures seek to focus attention on an aspect of thought about man and society which most scientists and philosophers happen to miss: that is, the effect of their thought in shaping the human and social reality itself. Man's thought about himself and society is not causally ineffective. The past civilisations, in this context, are treated as the result of the ways in which men conceived of themselves and society and the two of the most significant among them, the Indian and the Western, are singled out and discussed as paradigmatic cases.

The Concept of Society

What we confront as society is not something given by nature but rather that which was crafted by men in the past and that which is being made and remade by men in the present. Neither in respect of human individual nor in respect of human society the denial of essence has every meant or perhaps could ever mean the absolute absence of all limits and constraints.

If it be true in any sense that man and society are deeply affected by the way we conceive them to be then it is an imperative duty to make ourselves and others aware of the value implications of our conceptions and hold implications ourselves responsible for the same.

There are two ways in which we ultimately conceive society to be. It may be convinced either as the last term our thought in terms of which we want to understand everything else or only as an intermediate term beyond which there are other terms to which it is instrumental or subservient in a final sense.

Society need not be conceived as the last term of human thought. In this perspective, then, society would be conceived as a facilitating mechanism so that the individual may pursue his trans-social needs.

The choice between the two ways of conceiving becomes a valuation choice also.

The Two Predicaments

The two ultimate ways in which we can conceive society in relation to the individuals that compose it, have just been elaborated upon. The decision between the two, is not to be made in terms of their adequacy to reflect some pre-existent reality, but rather in terms of what we want that reality to be either choice in the true human fashion, leads to its own predicament in which it involves the society and the individual who have opted, consciously or unconsciously, for that conception.

The view which conceives of society as the last term of our thought in terms of which and for which everything else is to be understood give rise to what elsewhere is called the socio-centric predicament". The predicament primarily results from viewing the human individual as having nothing in himself that he does not owe to society and therefore, of seeking the justification for each or his acts in terms of its social consequences. The individual is basically defined in this perspective as a social animal.

Man's humanity is thus seen as derived from his sociality and it is the process of socialisation which really humanises him in the strict sense of the term. Further, the individual is seen as something temporary which comes into being and passes away. What endures is the society of which he is a member. Society and the individuals who have opted, consciously or unconsciously for that conception.

The view which conceives of society as the last term of our thought in terms of which and for which everything else is to be understood gives rise to what elsewhere is called "the socio-centric predicament." The predicament primarily results from viewing the human individual as having nothing in himself that he does not owe to society and, therefore of seeking the justification for each of his acts in terms of its social consequences. The individual is basically defined in this perspective as a social animal. Man's humanity is thus seen as derived from his sociality and it is the process of socialisation which really humanises him in the strict sense of the term. Further, the individual is seen as something temporary which comes into being and passes away. What endures is the society of which he is a member.

The social-centric perspective which makes man conceive of himself and society in this way leads to the social-centric predicament in that the individual who is supposed to have nothing in himself which is not derived from society is simultaneously supposed to be burdened with the absolute responsibility for all that happens to society also. The Greek, the Christian and the Communist versions are merely variations on this one theme which lies at the heart of Western culture. Man is essentially and intrinsically responsible not just for his own self but for others and this is not because he is free and his actions have consequences for others but because he is social or communal at the very heart of his being and cannot be conceived as apart from them. It is Adam's sin that Christ has to redeem. But Christ, at least was the son of God. Not son in the vision of Marc. There, it is man conditioned by the society and the class into which he is born who is expected to usher in the reign of freedom and hold himself if he does not do so. For man to have such a burden of others actions on his shoulders is certainly to develop a sense of community, but it is a community more in guilt than in redemption.

As against this, in the other perspective Man may be seen basically as a transcendent being. His sociality is only an accidental feature which no more defines him than say, his erect posture. He is the son of God or perhaps, the God himself when Aristotle said that outside society, one is either a god or a beast, he was not giving alternatives which would create any dilemma fear the Atman-centric thinker. Man be seen obviously not a beast and it sociality is to be accidental then he must be a god and so he is in spite of all appearances to the contrary.

Society is ultimately secondary in this perspective. Man is essentially a social or rather trans-social in nature. The relationship with the other which is the heart of sociality is, thus, secondary also.

Society in an equivalent manner, is seen either as a facilitating instrument for the pursuit of man's a social or trans-social ends or as an obstruction to the realisation of one's transcendence from an essentially other-centred or socio-centric consciousness.

The conflict between the egoistic and the moral consciousness is a common property among all who have achieved any level of self-conscious awareness at all. But the conflict between the moral and the spiritual consciousness is known only to those who have heard the call of the transcendent spirit. Buddha leaving his wife, child and Kingdom may be taken as the paradigmatic example of such a situation. The world of social, political and familial obligations is given up at the call of something which the individual cannot quite clearly formulate even to himself. What is clear is the dissatisfaction which one has with one's own state of affairs and neat what one actually, wants or what one is going to get by the giving up of such obligations.

In the traditional story, Buddha is led to renounce the worldly obligations by the sight of something outside his own self. It is the sight of suffering, old age and death which makes him leave the world and not any dissatisfaction with his own psychically lived life. The Hindu on the other hand, would or at least should have renounced not because of any concern with the specific condition of some other human being but because of some condition of his own life. Buddha's return to save the suffering humanity to show it the way and to set in motion the wheel of dharma is non-Hindu in character. So is also the vow of seeking refuge in the religious community called the sangh society in the Atman-centric perspective therefore is seen only as a midway term of thought and not as the last term in terms of which everything else is to be understood and justified. It does help a person to get away from his ego-centred consciousness which is always concerned with the satisfaction of petty personal desires. The others in the Hindu tradition, includes not only persons, but ancestors, gods, plants, animals, earth, sky and so forth.

The idea of avatara in Hinduism and the ideal of bodhisatva in Buddhism seem obvious exceptions to what we have been trying to characterise as the Atman-centric traditions in India.

The Atman-centricity leads a people's attention away from an active concern with society and its betterment as much the consciousness which is centred on the enjoyment of its own hedonic or aesthetic states. When a society's best brains are concerned with the pursuit of something which is essentially a social or trans-social and which requires an active withdrawal from the institutions that sustain it, then, the road is prepared for the inevitable take-over either by those who are interested only in their own gain or by those who are bent on transforming the world in the image of their own good.

The intrinsically good have a natural impulse to withdraw from the social world, as the most meaningful things are usually realised outside it.

The two predicaments, then, derive from the two ways in which the relation between society and individual can be conceived. Each of the ways affects profoundly the direction in which a society, which conceives of itself in that way, moves and develops.

Perspectives of Freedom

Freedom is a word which has many meanings. The Problem, at least at one level, is not so much of freedom as of freedoms one's freedom seems to be essentially limited by the freedom of others and thus nobody can be free, for each is limited by the other.

The limitation on freedom arises, however, by the very fact of the multiplicity of persons in interaction. The fact that there is another centre of freedom with whom one is in some sort of an active inter-relationship leads essentially to the limitation of one's freedom. There seems an invariability about the fact that the problem of freedom may only be resolved by giving up the dream of absolute freedom and accepting the limitation of one freedom by another.

Is absolute freedom not possible in a situation where there are not only natural constraints but multiple centres of freedom?

The Faustian (i.e., without barriers) quest for freedom and power has been supposed to be a specific characteristic of the Western man and his culture. But it has rarely been noted that the Hindu quest is also for infinite freedom and power, though conceived in a different sense. The extroverted Faustian seeking of Western man can only be realised through the annihilation of the freedom of all others except oneself. The seeking for infinite freedom and power has, therefore to be conceived in such a way that its realisation in absolute terms by one person does not conflict with its equal realisation in absolute terms by another.

The thinking about freedom has a long tradition both in India and the West. But in the West, somehow, freedom has always been thought of in relation to action whether it be the action which is not done under constraint of anyone else or action which is in accordance with an external (law) or internal (moral) or internal-external norms.

The action may even be conceived apart from these norms whether internal or external or both and thought of in terms of its seeking the satisfaction of reference to any norms whatsoever. What one is actually able to do depends not only another human beings but also on the state of one's psychophysical organism. If freedom them, is to depend solely on oneself, it cannot be considered as centering in action but rather in willing or even in intention. The famous dictum of Kant that nothing in the world can be called good without qualification except a Good will derives, most probably from such considerations. The stories are the other great group in the Western tradition who have envisaged freedom in terms of willing rather than action.

This is perhaps the farthest that Western thought has gone in the direction of conceiving freedom as an internal state unrelated to anything outside itself. But even here freedom, though unrelated to society and specific circumstances, is conceived of in terms of willing according to a norm. Fundamentally, both will and intention are concerned with the achievement of some state of affairs relating to persons, situations or things. However, in both cases, freedom is conceived of in relation to something external which is sought or desired to be achieved.

As against this, the Indian conceives of freedom in a totally different way for him freedom has got nothing to do with action. It is rather a state of being or consciousness which because it is free, is intrinsically joyous and blissful in its very nature. Complete liberation or moksa, therefore, is usually defined as that where even the possibility of suffering lapses or ceases. The outside includes not merely others but one's own body and mind as we, Freedom is a state of continuously enjoyed consciousness which does not seek any end whatsoever and whose freedom is an immediately felt reality expressing itself in the twin facts of being calm and joyous, on the one hand, and of being essentially unaffected by anything else, on the other. The latter fact does not mean that one becomes incapable of entering into any relation with the other but rather, in K.C. Bhattacharya's classic phrase in relating oneself to the other without getting related. The point obviously is that one's freedom is not affected in any way by the relationship with the other into which also one enters because of one's freedom.

The very concept of the other however, may also be denied, and this has actually been done in powerful school of Indian tradition. The exercise of the will presupposes the other and thus even in this respect the West tends to differentiate itself from India. As far as the denial of the other is concerned, there is no such absolute denial in the West as in the advaitic tradition. What is attempted to be denied there is not the reality or actuality of the other but rather his freedom.

The advaitic denial of the other, however, operates only on the plane of the transcendent where the modalities of space, time and causality become completely irrelevant. It is because of this that each person may realise this absolute for himself without in any way affecting the realisation of the same absolute by others.

At the empirical plane, such a conception of freedom can translate itself into reality only by a perpetual process of each trying to subjugate the other to his own will as far as possible. The conflict between individuals will be within the groups rather than outside them.

At the transcendental plane, on the other hand the elimination of the other is to be achieved at the psychic level of conscious awareness.

It has nothing to do with one's relationships to others at the empirical level except that they should be least possible in number and of such a nature as to avoid one's being disturbed by them.

The history of the two traditions, Western and Indian, supports to a great extent the different deflective which the two concepts of freedom history does not show a struggle between groups for mastery or individuals for supremacy within a group but this struggle, however fierce and prolonged, has seldom been ideologically oriented as in the West. Only the individual psyche is the seat of genuine value conflicts, for in it alone can ultimate freedom be actualised.

The history of the West on the other hand, is essentially temporal and empirical in character. Men and groups are the embodiment of values and their social conflicts, the conflicts between values and ideals of different kinds. However, the concept of dharma-yuddha elaborated in both the Ramayana and the Mahabharata may be thought of as a standing disconfirmation of much this thesis. Three things may be said in this connection.

First, the Philosophic reflection that this problem of dharma-yuddha or righteous war gave rise to strikes at the very roots of all empirical action, or anything else.

Secondly, it may be interesting to note that the task of establishing the reign of righteousness was left to the Lord. The people could only suffer and pray.

Thirdly, even it be agreed that the establishment of a righteous society was the duty of the people, specially Ksatriyas, the people belonging to the warrior-caste the concept of a righteous society basically was that which permitted or rather did not interfere with the pursuit of transcendental freedom. The view of freedom as transcendental and a social is not compromised at all.

The recognition of the individual wandering mendicants who was theoretically dead to the society, its societal and familial obligations, and who was not even supposed to have a father or mother, brother or sister, as the highest was a recognition by the society of its own secondary character. The sannyasi, was a symbol for one who had given up the world for the pursuit of transcendental freedom.

The recognition by the society of the asocial and trans-social pursuit of the sannyasi and superior to any other that concerned empirical or social ends seems to have been a fact. Similarly, it seems to have been accepted that it was the supreme duty of society to facilitate such a pursuit. The only parallel that can be thought of to such a situation in the Western tradition seems to relate itself to aesthetic values in the nineteenth century. In the last half of this century, the arts sought their independence in the cult of art fear arts sake and many of the artists become some sort of self-conscious a social beings. Yet, though a social, the artist and his activity came to be recognised by society itself as something superior and infinitely valuable to it.

The parallel, however, does not go very far. The idea of an asocial or trans-social activity which yet is recognised by society as superior obligation to foster, promote and facilitate goes so much against the deepest stand of Western thought that it cannot accept it for very long without feeling guilty about it.

The basic contrast in the conception of freedom, that, may be delineated in terms of freedom as a state of being and freedom as that which is essentially related to action.

The idea of maximising freedom and achieving it through social policy, however, involves the notion that freedom is the sort of thing that can be measured and about which it can significantly be said that it has increased or decreased.

4

Women Rights and Plight

The problem regarding women rights in India is not primarily lack of legislation on the issue, per se. We have the most well thought out and well defined Constitution in the whole world. Our legislature has been very efficient in comprehensively legislating on almost all women centric issues. The real lacunae lies in the implementation of these rights. Moreover, we need to create awareness among females about the rights that they have been accorded. This awareness needs to be created among the lower strata of the society in particular. Most of the women in our country are not even aware of their rights. They readily subject themselves to suppression unaware of the provisions that have been made just to enable them to lead a better life.

According to our Constitution, a female has the following rights:-

1. Right to education
2. Right to equality
3. Right to freedom of speech and expression
4. Right to information
5. Right to nutrition
6. Right to health and care
7. Right to protection from abuse and exploitation
8. Right to work
9. Right to fair wages or equal pay

10. Right to recreation
11. Right to name and nationality
12. Right to vote
13. Right to follow any religion
14. Reproductive rights
15. Right to constitutional remedies

Still how many of the above mentioned rights are actually exercised by women in our country or rather how many of these rights are they actually "allowed" to know and practise? Not even half of them.

To add to the misery, crimes against women have doubled over the past ten years, according to the latest data released by the National Crime Records Bureau (NCRB). As many as 2.24 million crimes against women were reported over the past decade: 26 crimes against women are reported every hour, or one complaint every two minutes!

Cruelty by husbands and relatives under Section 498-A of Indian Penal Code (IPC) is the major crime committed against women across the country, with 909,713 cases reported over the past 10 years, or 10 every hour.

Assault on women with the intent to outrage her modesty, earlier classified as molestation under Section 354 of IPC, is the second most reported crime against women over the last decade with 470,556 cases reported.

Kidnapping and abduction of women (315,074) is the third most reported crime followed by rape (243,051), insult to modesty of women (104,151) and dowry death (80,833).

More than 66,000 cases have been reported under the Dowry Prohibition Act, 1961, over the last decade. Ten cases of cruelty by husband and relatives are reported every hour across the country.

NCRB added three more heads under which cases of crime against women were reported in 2014. These include attempt to commit rape (4,234), abetment of suicide of women (3,734) under Section 306 IPC and protection of women from domestic violence (426).

As many as 66 per cent women reported being sexually harassed by their male counterparts around 2-5 times, during the past year, a 2010 study in New Delhi had found.

The appalling reality is that all the aforementioned crimes are punishable offences in India, yet the sinister acts are increasing in number with each passing year. Moreover, most cases of domestic violence, dowry deaths, rapes, cruelty by husband and relatives, outraging of modesty, are not even reported to the police due to being unaware of their rights and more so, due to societal pressures which compel the victim to allow her offender to go scot-free and lead a normal life.

An interesting thing to do here would be to discuss in brief the rights of the transgenders in our country, their plight and to see how are their rights and status different from that of women.

Racial Equality, Religious Freedom, Freedom of Speech

These are the things that often come to mind when we speak of human rights. But on the international stage, rights for certain communities are often disregarded. The transgender people in the developing world is one such example.

Hijras have a recorded history of more than 4,000 years. Ancient myths bestow them with special powers to bring luck and fertility. Sadly, despite this supposedly sanctioned place in Indian culture, hijras face severe harassment and discrimination in every walk of life. Deepa, a 72 years old hijra living in Mumbai says: "Nobody says, "I'd love to be a hijra!" Not if they know what happens to us. But what else can we do? A hijra has a man's body, but the soul is a woman."

In India, there are approximately one million transgender people. Hijras—physiological males who take on a feminine gender identity—comprise one segment of the transgender population. On the one hand, hijras are called upon to offer special blessings during auspicious occasions like weddings and birth ceremonies, while on the other, they are not only ignored but are often ostracized from the society. Discrimination has prevented most hijras from obtaining decent education, jobs and housing. The majority of transgender Indians live in slums and, with limited job opportunities, resort to sex work or begging. Though some transgender Indians receive funding for HIV-prevention, most are excluded from receiving basic support for their livelihoods because they are typecast as a "high risk" population.

The uphill struggle for the hijras first begins with finding acceptance within the family. "My family didn't know I was castrated," tells Chandini, 28. "My hijra friends teased me because I still went home in men's clothes, so I decided to go home as I am. When I got there some people in the street spotted me and told my mother, "Here's your son!" She saw me and fainted. My father came, he said, "I don't have a son, go away!" I said, "I'm not your son, I'm your daughter now.""'

On unveiling the truth, hijras are usually forced to leave their family. Yet, the society they take refuge in, is equally unwelcoming. Until recently, Hijras had few rights and weren't recognised by Indian law. This denied them the right to vote, the right to own property, the right to marry and the right to claim formal identity through any official documents such as a passport or driving licence. Accessing healthcare, employment or education was almost impossible. In the face of such odds they are forced to earn money any way they can. "In the day we go around the shops and beg," says Deepa. "They give us a rupee each and we go away. Sometimes we dance at weddings and festivals, we can get good money from this."

Since 2006, hijras in the state of Bihar have been employed by the government as tax collectors, singing loudly about the debt outside the defaulter's premises until they are shamed into paying up "one of the most effective tax recovery methods ever used in India." Yet, for many hijras the method of making ends is prostitution.

As is the case for all gay, lesbian and bisexual people living in India, simply by being sexually active hijras are said to break the law. Section 377 of the Indian Penal Code (IPC) outlaws any "carnal intercourse against the order of nature" "in other words, any sex that is not between a man and a woman with the aim of reproduction. Brought in by the British in 1860 to try and curb the "heathen customs" of the local population, it carries with it a potential life sentence.

While attitudes in the UK have matured considerably and such legislation has long since been removed from the British statute books, it still remained rooted in the Indian system until recently. Shockingly, sometimes the police personnel, gangs of local thugs known as "goondas" frequently rob and sexually assault hijras on the street. These attacks are rarely prevented or reported by the locals, since, they themselves have apprehensions about the hijras and are more often than not, "scared" of them.

Until very recently these attitudes were reflected and strengthened by the Indian media which itself seemed to suffer from a certain amount of gender vertigo. Hijras were routinely portrayed as wily tricksters who led unsuspecting men astray or half-man half-woman freak shows, almost devilish in their customs and practices. In 2003, an HIV/AIDS and human rights research centre in Lucknow was raided and the coordinator jailed under IPC 377 for "conspiracy to promote homosexual activities". An English language newspaper ran the headline: *Gay Racket Busted- 2 NGOs Caught in the Act.*

While transgender Indians continue to face discrimination, they have also made significant social and legal gains. The States of Tamil Nadu and Kerala in India were the first to introduce a transgender (hijra/ aravani) welfare policy. According to which, transgender people could access free Sex Reassignment Surgery (SRS) in the Government Hospital (only for MTF); free housing programme; various citizenship documents; admission in government colleges with full scholarship for higher studies; alternative sources of livelihood through formation of self-help groups (for savings) and initiating income-generation programmes (IGP). Tamil Nadu was also the first state to form a Transgender Welfare Board with representatives from the transgender community. In 2016, Kerala started implementing free SRS through government hospitals. "The Truth about Me: A Hijra Life Story" by Transgender A. Revathi is part of the syllabus for Final Year students of The American College in Madurai. The American College is the first college in India to introduce Third Gender literature and studies for genderqueer people was coined in this college by gender activist Gopi Shankar.

In November 2009, transgender people won the right to be listed as "other" rather than "male" or "female" on electoral rolls and voter identity card. More so, in October 2010, the Karnataka state government approved that transgender citizens become eligible for government seed funding to start self-employment ventures—a change catalysed by AJWS's grantee, the Salaam Initiative. Hijras were factored into the government's policy-making for the first time when they were named as a target group for a breakthrough de-addiction programme. In the same month the State of Tamil Nadu allowed hijras, if they wish, to be recognised as "T" rather than just "M" or "F" on ration cards with the same being planned soon for passports and driving licences. Indian Census had never recognised third gender while collecting census data for years. But in 2011, data of Transgender's were collected with details related to their employment, Literacy and Caste. In India, total population of transgender is around 4.88 lakh as per 2011 census.

On 15th April 2014, Supreme Court of India declared transgender people as a socially and economically backward class entitled to reservations in receiving education and jobs, and also directed union and state governments to frame welfare schemes for them.

On 24th April 2015, the Rajya Sabha passed the Rights of Transgender Persons Bill, 2014 guaranteeing rights and entitlements, reservations in education and jobs (two per cent reservation in government jobs), legal aid, pensions, unemployment allowances and skill development for transgender people. It also contains provisions to prohibit discrimination in employment, prevent abuse, violence and exploitation of transgender people. The Bill also provides for the establishment of welfare boards at the Centre and State level, and for Transgender Rights Courts. Social Justice and Empowerment Minister Thaawar Chand Gehlot stated on 11th June 2015, that the Government would introduce a comprehensive Bill for transgender rights. According to Mr Gehlot, the Government intends to provide transgender people with all rights and entitlements currently enjoyed by Scheduled Castes and Scheduled Tribes.

With the aforementioned legislations in place now, we can hope for amelioration in the condition and status of the transgenders. It is imperative that they are considered to be as much an essential part of the society as any other gender. They should be accommodated in the society from the very beginning of their lives, like admitting them into conventional schools. This would even help lessen the fear and apprehensions fabricated in the minds of the general public at large against the transgenders. Fortunately, something, is beginning to alter in the traditional Indian mindset as presently there seem to be appreciable changes taking place in terms of how this group is being treated and recognised by mainstream society. Ela Gandhi has correctly observed that, "A law alone cannot solve the problems of society, the attitude of the people needs to change" and to win the battle against the ostracisation and discrimination of the transgender community, we need to bring change in the mind set of the people.

5

Crimes Against Women: Top Five States

Andhra Pradesh leads in crimes against women with almost 263,839 cases reported, over the past decade. The state statistics of crimes committed are as follows:

1. Insult to modesty of women- 35,733 cases
2. Cruelty by husband and relatives- 117,458 cases
3. Assault on women with the intent to outrage her modesty- 51,376 cases
4. Dowry-related deaths- 5,364 cases

West Bengal is second with 239,760 cases reported related to:

1. Cruelty by husband and relatives -152,852
2. Kidnapping and abduction- 27,371
3. Dowry-related deaths – 4,891

Uttar Pradesh ranks third (236,456), followed by Rajasthan (188,928) and Madhya Pradesh (175,593).

These five States account for almost half of all the crimes committed against women across the country over the last decade.

Kidnapping and abduction of women has gone up by 264 per cent, a more than three-fold increase, over the past decade, from 15,750 cases in 2005 to 57,311 cases in 2014. Uttar Pradesh is the worst affected State with 58,953 cases.

Police investigations have found that in places like Delhi, Agra, Madhya Pradesh and Rajasthan, denotified tribes (also known as criminal tribes), such as Bedia, Nat, Kanjar and Banjara, are involved in kidnapping minor girls, according to a report by the United Nations (UN).

These tribes raise kidnapped girls as their own daughters and then send them to Mumbai and Middle East to work in dance bars, brothels and escort services.

Madhya Pradesh reported the highest number of rape cases in the last decade being 34,143, followed by West Bengal (19,993), Uttar Pradesh (19,894), Maharashtra (19,177) and Rajasthan (18,654).

Around 35 per cent of women, globally, have experienced either physical or sexual intimate partner violence or non-partner sexual violence, according to a 2013 global review by UN Women.

Some national violence studies show that up to 70 per cent of women have experienced physical or sexual violence in their lifetime, from an intimate partner, the UN report said.

Sixty-five per cent of Indian men believe that women should tolerate violence in order to keep the family together, and women sometimes deserve to be beaten.[6] In January 2011, the IMAGES Questionnaire reported that 24 per cent of Indian men had committed sexual violence at some point during their lives.

In order to ameliorate the predicament of women, we need to analyse and conceptualise the meaning of society, freedom, liberty, morals, ethics and rights.

6

Social Evils and Violence Against Women in India

1. RAPE- It is one of the most common crimes committed against women in India. ***Criminal Law Amendment Act, 2013*** defines rape as penile and non-penile penetration in bodily orifices of a woman by a man, without her consent. In India, a woman is raped every 29 minutes.[7] It is punishable under Section 376 of the IPC.

Women are becoming more independent and educated these days, which in turn is increasing their likelihood to report their rape. Although rapes are becoming frequently reported, many go unreported or the complaints are withdrawn due to the perception of family honour being compromised. Women often do not receive justice because police often does not give them a fair hearing, and/or medical evidence is often unrecorded which makes it easy for offenders to get away with their crimes under the current laws.[8]

However, increased attention in the media, after the ***Delhi gang rape case***, is successfully creating awareness among the public and also helping empower women to report the crime.

2. Child Marriage-According to the Indian law, it is a marriage where either the girl is below 18 years of age or the boy is below 21 years of age. Child marriages are prohibited and punishable under ***The Prohibition of Child Marriage Act, 2006.*** UNICEF considers child marriage to be a violation of human rights. According to the 2001 Census there are 1.5 million girls in India under the age of 15 years who are already married.

Some of the adverse consequences of child marriage are that the child losses out on education opportunities, becomes vulnerable to domestic violence, faces sexual exploitation, early pregnancy and health risks, higher infant mortality rate, low weight babies, pre-mature births etc.[9]

Nagi[10], in 1993, suggested that the practice of dowry creates a fear and pressure to avoid late marriages, hence, encouraging early marriages.

Poverty in India has been cited as a cause of early marriages. Child marriage of girls is a way out of desperate economic conditions, and way to reduce the expenses of a poor family.[11]

3. Domestic Violence-Domestic violence is abuse by one partner against another in an intimate relationship such as dating, marriage, cohabitation or a familial relationship (example; mother, sister). The Indian Government has taken measures to try to reduce domestic violence through legislation such as the ***Protection of Women from Domestic Violence Act 2005 (DVA).***

According to the DVA, 2005, there are five types of exploitation and all of them are actionable under the said law:-

1. Physical exploitation
2. Verbal exploitation
3. Sexual exploitation
4. Mental exploitation
5. Economic exploitation

4. Dowry- Dowry is a practice prevalent in India, where the bride's family transfers wealth or property to the groom. It is basically a consideration for marriage, demanded by the groom's family. Such act of giving and taking of dowry is prohibited and punishable under the ***Dowry Prohibition Act, 1961.***

Dowry system has somewhat been done away with in contemporary India, but unfortunately it hasn't been abolished altogether. Despite all the fetters imposed on dowry, the presence of this malpractice can still be felt in some traditions and cultures. Heavy amount of considerations are still paid to the groom and his family in the form of "gifts" and the bride does not oppose this in the name of it being a part of their customs and traditions. The unfortunate part being that such practices are sometimes prevalent among the most educated of families. However, they tend to forget that the act of giving as well as taking or demanding dowry is an act punishable under the law and hence, by propagating this dowry system, they unknowingly become perpetrators of crime.

5. Sex Determination- ***Pre-Natal Diagnostic Techniques Act, 1994*** prohibits determination and disclosure of the sex of the foetus. It makes sex determination a punishable offence.

Female foeticide as well as female infanticide are crimes punishable under Sections 315 and 316 of the IPC as well.

6. Acid Attacks- Acid attack is the act of throwing acid or an alternative corrosive substance onto a person's body with the intention to disfigure, maim, torture or kill. It has been made a punishable offence under Section 326 A of the IPC, recently.

Compared to women throughout the world, women in India are at a higher risk of being victims of acid attacks. In 2010, there was a high of 27 reported cases of chemical assaults. Scholars believe that acid attacks in India are being under-reported. Thirty-four per cent of acid attacks in India have been determined to be related to rejection of marriage or refusal by a women of sexual advances. Twenty per cent of acid attacks have been related to land, property and/or business disputes. Acid attacks related to marriage are often spurred by dowry disagreements.[12]

7. Sexual Harassment at Workplace-The opening years of this century have witnessed an increasing proportion of women in the workforce. Even though it is expected that more women will enter the workplace, we find that workplaces have largely ignored the different and specific needs of women and continue to be male oriented. Attitudes, policies, systems, infrastructure and the environment within the workplace often reflect the prevalent mindsets within the larger society in their gender biases and stereotyped images of the roles that society expects men and women to play. Increased and continued participation of women is viable only if there exists a conducive and enabling environment for both women and men, based on the principles of equality, as enshrined in the Constitution of India, national legislations and ratification of international conventions that promote concepts of non-discrimination and equal opportunity. However, these principles need to find resonance in the practices, culture and systems embedded within an organisation.

Sexual harassment is not epidemic, it is pandemic- an everyday, everywhere occurrence (Susan Enrlich Martin, 'Sexual Harassment: The Link Between Gender Stratification, Sexuality and Women's Economic Status' in *Women,* JO Freeman (ed), 1984, p. 54). It is not an aberration, rather, it is an expression of the prevailing male view of women (Laura J Evan, ' Sexual Harassment: Women's Hidden Occupational Hazard' in *The Victimisation of Women*, Margaret Gates (ed), 1985, p. 221). Sexual harassment at work is the most oppressive form of sex discrimination that undercuts women's potential for independence and equality. It disrupts a woman's drive for autonomy outside the home and family by sexualising her work role and by making sexuality a condition of economic survival (Susan Enrlich Martin, 'Sexual Harassment: The Link Between Gender Stratification, Sexuality and Women's Economic Status' in *Women*, JO Freeman (ed), 1984, p. 54). Sexual harassment occurs at the intersection of social and economic inequalities by expressing the unequal social power of women, sexualising their subordination and deepening their "powerlessness" as women.

The problem of sexual harassment of women at workplace results in violation of the fundamental rights of a woman to equality under Articles 14 and 15 of the Constitution of India and her right to life and to live with dignity under Article 21 of the Constitution and right to practice any profession or to carry on any occupation, trade or business which includes a right to a safe environment free from sexual harassment.

The traditionally accepted patriarchal notion views men as the economic providers and women as inferior sex whose main role is tied to their reproductive capacities and sexuality. (Linda Wirth, 'Sexual Harassment at Work' in *Promoting Gender Equality at Work-Turning Vision into Reality,* 1997, p. 131). With modernisation, women have entered into the professional arena but have met with occupational segregation. Women are occupationally segregated as woman's place in occupational world is characterised by:

(1) Lower pay than men.

(2) Subordination to male superiors.

(3) Concentration in sex stereotyped occupations which requires the virtues of nurturing and caring, etc.

"The occupational segregation and sexual stereotyping contribute to sexual harassment of women employed in both traditionally 'female' and traditionally 'male' jobs through a phenomenon called sex role spillover. Sex role spillover occurs when gender based expectations for behaviour get carried into the workplace so that workers in their work roles are expected to behave as males or females. Men view the presence of women as an invasion of male economic turf (i.e., as a challenge to men's better pay and supervisory authority); an invasion of their social turf and a threat to their definition of their work and selves as masculine".[13] A national trade union in the Netherlands pointed out that sexual harassment "is not a temporary phenomenon because men feel threatened in their status and authority by women's improved access to the labour market". Stanley and Wise have commented, while referring to everyday life than the workplace: Sexual harassment therefore serves to keep women, and men, in our respective places; the places that men define as appropriate; and it also, serves so as to bring back into line, by force if necessary, any woman who departs from this or who doesn't fit in how she's supposed to be.

In India, till 1997, sexual harassment at workplace was not recognised by the legal system- neither in the form of legislative enactments, nor through the judicial interpretations by the courts. It was for the first time in 1997, that the legal scenario got changed due to judicial activism exhibited by the Supreme Court of India. To respect the fundamental rights of gender equality, to life and liberty, and the right to carry on the profession of one's own choice enshrined in Constitution of India and to fulfil the country's obligation under international instruments (The UN Convention on Elimination of All Forms of Discrimination Against Women was signed by India in 1979 and consequently ratified in 1993), the Supreme Court of

India pronounced a landmark decision – *Vishaka* vs. *State of Rajasthan* in the year 1997. In the absence of an enacted law to provide for effective enforcement of the basic human right of gender equality and guarantee against sexual harassment at workplace, the Supreme Court laid down certain guidelines in the *Vishaka* judgement for compliance at all workplaces and institutions.

The Supreme Court incorporated the definition as contained in the General Recommendation 23 to Art 11 of CEDAW relating to violence and equality in employment. The court further clarified that such conduct would be 'discriminatory to the woman' if it created a hostile working environment or if the woman had reasonable grounds to believe that her objection to such behaviour would affect her chances of promotion, or result in adverse consequences for her.

The Supreme Court of India gave new definition of sexual harassment of women at workplace in *Vishaka* vs. *State of Rajasthan*[14]. The case ruling establishes that sexual harassment violates a woman's rights in the workplace and is thus not just a matter of personal injury.

For this purpose, sexual harassment includes such unwelcome sexually determined behaviour (whether directly or by implication) as:

(a) Physical contact and advances;

(b) A demand or request for sexual favours;

(c) Sexually coloured remarks;

(d) Showing pornography;

(e) Any other unwelcome physical, verbal or non-verbal conduct of sexual nature.

Where any of these acts is committed in circumstances where under the victim of such conduct has a reasonable apprehension that in relation to the victim's employment or work whether she is drawing salary, or honorarium or voluntary, whether in government, public or private enterprise such conduct can be humiliating and may constitute a health and safety problem. It is discriminatory for instance when the woman has reasonable grounds to believe that her objection would disadvantage her in connection with her employment or work including recruiting or promotion or when it creates a hostile work environment. Adverse consequences might be visited if the victim does not consent to the conduct in question or raises any objection thereto. In *Medha Kotwal Lele* vs. *Union of India,*[15] Writ petition (Crl) no. 173-177/1999; several petitions were filed that in respect of sexual harassment cases, the complaints committees were not formed in the concerned offices, departments etc, in accordance with the guidelines issued by the apex court in Vishaka case.

In *Apparel Export Promotion Council* vs. *AK Chopra*[16], the Supreme Court stated: each incident of sexual harassment, at the place of work, results in violation of the fundamental right to life and liberty- the two most precious fundamental rights guaranteed by the Constitution of India. As early as in 1993 at the ILO Seminar held at Manila, it was recognised that sexual harassment of women at work place was a form of 'gender discrimination against women'.

United States

The Civil Rights Act of 1964, title VII prohibits sex discrimination in workplaces. The U.S. government body that enforces the Civil Rights Act, the Equal Employment Opportunity Commission (EEOC), defines sexual harassment as

"[u]nwelcome sexual advances, requests for sexual favours, and other verbal or physical conduct of a sexual nature," when

(1) submission to such conduct is made either explicitly or implicitly a term or condition of an individual's employment;

(2) submission to or rejection of such conduct by an individual is used as the basis for employment decisions affecting such individual; or

(3) such conduct has the purpose or effect of unreasonably interfering with an individual's work performance or creating an intimidating, hostile or offensive working environment. The court said in *Burlington Industries* vs. *Ellerth*[17], and *Faragher* vs. *City of Boca Raton*[18]:

(a) An employer can be held liable for sexual misconduct by supervisors, whether or not the employer knew about it; and whether or not the employee suffered adverse job consequences for refusing a supervisor's unwelcome advances.

(b) An employer may be liable for both negligent and intentional torts committed by an employee within the scope of his or her employment.

Similarly, the United Kingdom enacted the **EQUALITY Act 2010**. The Act legally protects people from discrimination in the workplace and in wider society.

It replaced previous anti-discrimination laws with a single Act, making the law easier to understand and strengthening protection in some situations. It sets out the different ways in which it's unlawful to treat someone. Before the Act came into force there were several pieces of legislation to cover discrimination, including:

(1) Sex Discrimination Act 1975

(2) Race Relations Act 1976

(3) Disability Discrimination Act 1995

Equality Act provisions which came into force on 1 October 2010:

(1) the basic framework of protection against direct and indirect discrimination, harassment and victimisation in services and public functions, premi, work, education, associations and transport;

(2) changing the definition of gender reassignment, by removing the requirement for medical supervision;

(3) providing protection for people discriminated against because they are perceived to have, or are associated with someone who has, a protected characteristic;

(4) clearer protection for breastfeeding mothers;

(5) applying a uniform definition of indirect discrimination to all protected characteristics;

(6) harmonising provisions allowing voluntary positive action.

Provisions relating to work specifically were as follows:

(1) allowing claims for direct gender pay discrimination where there is no actual comparator;

(2) making pay secrecy clauses unenforceable;

(3) extending protection in private clubs to sex, religion or belief, pregnancy and maternity, and gender reassignment;

(4) introducing new powers for employment tribunals to make recommendations which benefit the wider workforce.

Sexual harassment at the workplace is a universal problem. Even though the occurrence of sexual harassment at the workplace is widespread in India and elsewhere, this is the first time it has been recognised as an infringement of the fundamental rights of a woman, under Article 19(1)(g) of the Constitution of India "to practice any profession or to carry out any occupation, trade or business." Most international women's human rights movements have raised their voice against abuse and violence perpetrated against women in general. In 1979, the UN General Assembly adopted the **Convention on the Elimination of all forms of Discrimination Against Women (CEDAW).** Areas where discrimination was found to be rampant include political rights, marriage, family and employment. The convention emphasised that discrimination and attacks on a woman's dignity violated the principle of equality of rights.

The Sexual Harassment of Women at Workplace (Prevention, Prohibition and Redressal) Act, 2013 ensures that women are protected against sexual harassment at all the workplaces, be it in public or private. This will contribute to realisation of their right to gender equality, life and liberty and equality in working conditions everywhere. The sense of security at the workplace will improve women's participation in work, resulting in their economic empowerment and inclusive growth.

Before this Act of 2013, there was no Act in force which directly dealt with sexual harassment of women at workplace. After the Judgment pronounced by the Supreme Court of India in Vishaka case, the Bill was first introduced by women and child development minister Krishna Tirath in 2007 and approved by the Union Cabinet in January 2010. It was presented in the Lok Sabha in December 2010 and referred to the Parliamentary Standing Committee on Human Resources Development. The committee's report was published on 30th November 2011. In May 2012, the Union Cabinet approved an Amendment to include domestic workers. The amended Bill was finally passed by the Lok Sabha on 3rd September 2012. The Bill was passed by the Rajya Sabha on 26th February 2013. It received the assent of the President of India and was published in the Gazette of India, Extraordinary, Part-II, Section-1, dated the 23rd April 2013 as Act No. 14 of 2013.

The Act defines sexual harassment at the workplace and creates a mechanism for redressal of complaints. It also provides safeguards against false or malicious charges. The definition of "aggrieved woman", who will get protection under the Act is extremely wide to cover all women, irrespective of her age or employment status, whether in the organised or unorganised sectors, public or private and covers clients, customers and domestic workers as well. While the "workplace" in the Vishaka Guidelines is confined to the traditional office set-up where there is a clear employer-employee relationship, the Act goes much further to include organisations, department, office, branch unit etc. In the public and private sector, organised and unorganised, hospitals, nursing homes, educational institutions, sports institutes, stadiums, sports complex and any place visited by the employee during the course of employment including the transportation. Every employer is required to constitute an Internal Complaints Committee at each office or branch with 10 or more employees. The District Officer is required to constitute a Local Complaints Committee at each district, and if required at the block level. The Complaints Committee have the powers of civil courts for gathering evidence. The Complaints Committees are required to provide for conciliation before initiating an inquiry, if requested by the complainant. Penalties have been prescribed for employers. The Committee is required to complete the inquiry within a time period of 90 days. On completion of the inquiry, the report will be sent to the employer or the District Officer, as the case may be, they are mandated to take action on the report within 60 days. Non-compliance with the provisions of the Act shall be punishable with a fine of up to rupees 50,000. Repeated violations may lead to higher penalties and cancellation of licence or registration to conduct business.

7

The Sexual Harassment of Women at Workplace (Prevention, Prohibition and Redressal) Act, 2013

An Act to provide protection against sexual harassment of women at workplace and for the prevention and redressal of complaints of sexual harassment and for matters connected therewith or incidental thereto.

In this Act unless the context otherwise requires:-

(a) "aggrieved woman" means –

  (i) in relation to a workplace, a woman, of any age whether employed or not, who alleges to have been subjected to any act of sexual harassment by the respondent;

  (ii) in relation to a dwelling place or house, a woman of any age who is employed in such a dwelling place or house; (n) "sexual harassment" includes any one or more of the following unwelcome acts or behaviour (whether directly or by implication) namely:-

    (i) physical contact and advances; or

    (ii) a demand or request for sexual favours; or

    (iii) making sexually coloured remarks; or

    (iv) showing pornography; or

    (v) any other unwelcome physical, verbal or non-verbal conduct of sexual nature:

Section 3 - **Prevention of sexual harassment**

(1) No woman shall be subjected to sexual harassment at any workplace.

(2) The following circumstances, among other circumstances, if it occurs or is present in relation to or connected with any act or behaviour of sexual harassment may amount to sexual harassment:-

(i) implied or explicit promise of preferential treatment in her employment; or

(ii) implied or explicit threat of detrimental treatment in her employment; or

(iii) implied or explicit threat about her present or future employment status; or

(iv) interference with her work or creating an intimidating or offensive or hostile work environment for her; or

(v) humiliating treatment likely to affect her health or safety.

Discrimination in Employment (UN report)-

Examination of state reports to human rights bodies show that even States that have consistently topped the UN human rights development and gender indices, have a gender pay gap across all sectors. Moreover, the take up rate for employment is, in almost all sectors, higher for men than women. Factoring in differences based on disability or origin, there are further disparities in work place participation. Much of this occurs despite there being laws in place guaranteeing equality in the work place.

Similarly the concluding observations of the CESCR report to Germany, echoed in a later set of recommendations of the Human Rights Committee, indicated concern and noted:

"Like the ILO, the Committee is concerned about the persisting impediments to women in German society, in terms of promotion in employment and equal wages for work of equal value, both in the private and public sectors, and especially in federal bodies and academic institutions, despite the efforts of the State party to give a new impetus to the equal participation of women in the Labour market."

Similarly of Luxembourg the CESCR noted:

> "with concern that women are still under-represented in the work force. While taking note that the disparities between wages of men and women have been reduced, the Committee also notes with concern that the current level of wage difference (women receiving 15 per cent lower wages than men) remains a matter of concern."

The fact that the same issues identified as problematic in the Norwegian, German and Luxembourg reports are also found in the CEDAW concluding observations to the report of Azerbaijan seems to indicate that there are common challenges facing women in the employment sector in many regions:

> "The Committee continues to be concerned about the occupational segregation between women and men in the labour market and the gap in their wages. The Committee is also concerned about the potential negative impact on women of the Labour Code, which appears to be overly protective of women as mothers and to restrict women's economic opportunities in a number of areas.

Night Work (UN Report)

Originally limitations on women's ability to participate in work in mines and at night were constructed as being for their "protection." These protections were enshrined in international instruments including the ILO Convention Concerning Night work of Women Industry. This was first concluded in 1919, revised in 1934 and also in 1948. It "provides protection" to women by limiting their participation in industry between the hours of 10 pm and 7 am. Article 1 provides: "Women without distinction as to age, cannot be employed at night in public or private undertakings except for members of their family." The ILO Convention Concerning Employment of Women in Underground Work of All Kinds, 1935.626. It provides that no female can be employed in underground work at any time (many State refused to accept these instruments because of their discriminatory nature).

Although well meant at the time, the instruments are now considered as being out of date, discriminatory, paternalistic and as stereotyping women. Specifically the ban on night work is criticised for assuming that women are home-makers and care-givers but not bread-winners. The exemption for working for family reflects expectations that women will work without pay for family and indeed suggests that this is not work at all. Perhaps crucially in employment terms is the fact that night work is paid at double the rate of day time employment thus denying women the right to participate in night work is tantamount to limiting their income earning opportunities. Similarly accusations of paternalism have been made about denying women the right to work in mines. States are criticised for making choices for women and again for limiting their work horizons. Although initially the ban was put in place for the protection of women's health and because it was felt that women should not be made to do work which may be potentially harmful or hinder their ability to reproduce, it is now argued that developments in medical knowledge should be reflected by the removal of these bars.

Women's confinement to dead end, low paying, sex typed jobs and their subordination to male superiors and employers make them systematically vulnerable to sexual coercion. At the same time, the sex role expectations of women as wives, mothers and sex objects get carried into the workplace and are used to coerce women economically. Equality in employment is seriously impaired when women are subjected to such gender specific violence. The great Nani Palkhivala lamented that "complexity is heaped upon complexity and the confusion becomes worse confounded, the avalanche of amendments only results in more litigation."

The situation with the current sexual harassment act is the same. On one hand, we finally have a proper Law defining sexual harassment at workplace and proper guidelines for everyone on how to deal with this sensitive issue, on the other hand, this Act protects the workforce of the organised sector, leaving behind the schools and universities students who are most prone to this brutal act are still out of its ambit.

Like Ela Gandhi said, "A law alone cannot solve the problems of society, the attitude of the people need to change" and to win the battle against the sexual harassment we need to bring change in the mindset of the people.

8

Exhilaration of Women in the Society

Situation of women in India has indubitably improved over the years. The legislature provides ample protection to the women in the form of rights and laws. Various organisations, such as the following, have also been formed to protect and empower women and children, under the supervision of the ***Ministry of Women and Child Development***:-

1. National Institute of Public Cooperation and Child Development.
2. National Commission for Women.
3. Rashtriya Mahila Kosh.
4. National Commission for Protection of Child Rights.
5. Central Adoption Resource Agency.
6. Central Social Welfare Board.

The broad mandate of the Ministry is to have holistic development of Women and Children. It formulates plans, policies and programmes; enacts/ amends legislations, guides and coordinates the efforts of both governmental as well as non-governmental organisations working in the field of women and child development. Besides this, the Ministry implements certain innovative programmes for women and children. These programmes cover welfare and support services, training for employment and income generation, awareness generation and gender sensitisation. These programmes play a complimentary role to the other general developmental programmes in the sectors of health, education, rural development etc. All these efforts are directed to ensure that women are empowered both economically and socially, thus, become equal partners in national development along with men.

Evaluation of the Problem

Despite the presence of legislations, organisations, NGOs working for the welfare of women, what is amiss in the development of women in India?

On interacting with several females from different backgrounds, I learnt that most females were unaware of the rights and remedies available to them. The oblivion state prevailed more among the uneducated and poor women than their educated and affluent counterparts. So, making women about their rights would be the first step towards changing their predicament.

Most of us learn about our laws and rights at length in college. The need of the hour is to spread legal and fundamental rights awareness at primary school level itself. Workshops should be conducted about women and child rights, both in government as well as in private schools. So that it is embedded in the minds of young females from the beginning that they don't have to lead vegetative lives. They should be made aware about the existing laws and also the presence of NGOs formed for their help. A lot of states have helpline numbers for women now. Such numbers should be spread amongst all females. In fact, all states across the country should be mandated to have active helpline numbers for women and children.

Further, NGOs, people with legal know-how, should conduct similar workshops in small villages, towns along with the metropolitan cities. Women who do not have access to education must also receive the message and be empowered. Such campaigns should be conducted in every village, district, town and city of every state in the country. Similarly, such workshops should be conducted periodically in the corporate as well as the government offices, so as to inform the working women of their rights.

Another relevant step in this regard would be conducting self-defence classes for girls in all schools, whether public or private, aided or unaided. Such classes should be made a part of the curriculam mandatorily. This would empower the females and give them a sense of strength, making them fearless. Girls would no longer be perceived to be docile and weak, both by the society and also by their own selves. This would enhance their sense of liberty and freedom. Such a step might be useful in bringing down the acts of domestic and sexual violence against women!

It has been seen a lot of times that many cases of violence against women go unreported due to the fear of family name being harmed and compromised. It is often seen that the Panchayats are a little patriarchal in their approach and decisions, hence, women hesitate in approaching them. By Art. 247 power is reserved to the Parliament by law to provide for establishment of courts for better administration of laws made by the Parliament or of any existing laws with regard to the matters enumerated in the Union List, but no such courts have been constituted. In order to overcome this debacle, an informal dispute redressal mechanism should be set up in every block, by the government, having the force of law, which would in turn report to the district courts. Such mechanisms would deal with matters pertaining to dowry, domestic violence, child marriage, female foeticide and female infanticide. Maintaining the anonymity of the complainant would help in encouraging more female victims to record their cases.

9

Two Concepts of Liberty

— Sir Isaiah Berlin

To coerce a man is to deprive him of freedom. Like happiness and goodness, like nature and reality, the meaning of this term is so porous that there is little interpretation that it seems able to resist. Berlin proposes to examine no more than two of these senses –but those central ones, with a great deal of human history behind them. The first of these political senses of freedom or liberty, Berlin calls the 'negative sense', is involved in the answer to the question 'what is the area within which the subject- a person or group of person- is or should be left to do or be what he is able to do or be, without interference by other persons?'

The 'positive' conception of freedom as self-mastery, with its suggestion of a man divided against himself, has in fact and as a matter of the history of doctrines and of practice, splitting of personality into two: the transcendent, dominant controller, and passions to be disciplined and brought to heel.

Berlin emphasises negative liberty over positive liberty.

The 'positive sense', is involved in the answer to the question 'What, or who is the source of control or interference that can determine someone to do, or be, one thing rather than another?'

The Notion of Negative Freedom

I am normally said to be free to the degree to which no human being interferes with my activity. Political liberty in this sense is simply the area within which a man can act unobstructed by others. If I am prevented by other persons from doing what I could otherwise do, I am to that degree unfree; and if this area is contracted by other men beyond a certain minimum, I can be described as being coerced, or may be, enslaved. Coercion, however, does not cover every kind of inability. It implies the deliberate interference of other human beings in the area in which I could act. If I say that I am unable to jump more than 10 feet in the air, or cannot read because I am blind, it would be eccentric to say that I am to that degree enslaved or coerced. Mere incapacity to attain a goal is not lack of political freedom. This is brought out by the use of such modern expressions as 'economic freedom' and its counterpart, 'economic slavery'. It is argued, very plausibly, that if a man is too poor to afford something on which there is no legal ban- a loaf of bread, a journey round the world, recourse to the law courts- he is as little free to have it as he would be if it were forbidden to him by law. If my poverty were a kind of disease, which prevented me from buying bread or paying for the journey round the world, this inability would not naturally be described as a lack of freedom, least of all political freedom. This use of the term depends on a particular social and economic theory about the causes of my poverty or weakness. If my lack of material means is due to my lack of mental or physical capacity, then I begin to speak of being deprived of freedom cannot simply of poverty only if one accepts the theory. If in addition, one believer that he is being kept in what by a specific arrangement which we consider unjust or unfair, we speak of economic slavery or oppression. 'The nature of things does not madden us, only ill will does, said Rousseau. The criterion of oppression is the past that I believe to be played by other human beings, directly or indirectly, with or without the intention of doing so. By being free in his senses I mean not being interfered with by others. The wider the area of non-interference the wider my freedom.

This is what the classical English political philosophers meant when they used this word. They disagreed about how wide the area could or should be. Because they perceived, that human purposes and activities do not automatically harmonise with one another; and, because they put high value on other goals, such as justice, or happiness, or culture, or security, or varying degrees of equality, they were prepared to curtail freedom in the interests of other values and indeed, of freedom itself. Consequently, it is assumed, by these thinkers that the area of men's free action must be limited by law. But equally it is assumed, especially by such libertarians as Locke and Mill in England and Constant and Tocqueville in France, that there ought to exist a certain minimum area of personal freedom which must on no account be violated; for if it is overstepped, the individual will find himself in an area too narrow for even that minimum development of his natural faculties which alone makes it possible to pursue, and even to conceive, the various ends which men hold good or right or sacred. If follows that a frontier must be drawn between the area of private life and that of public authority. Men are largely interdependent and no man's activity is so completely private as never to obstruct the lives of others in anyway. 'Freedom for the pike is death for the minnows'.

The liberty of some must depend on the restraint of others.

Philosophers with an optimistic view of human nature, and a belief in the possibility of harmonising human interest, such as Locke or Adam Smith's, in some moods, Mill, believed that social harmony and progress were compatible with reserving a large area for private life over which neither the state nor any other authority must be allowed to trespass. Hobbes and those who agreed with him, like conservative or reactionary thinkers, argued that if men were to be prevented from destroying one another and making social life a jungle, greater safeguards must be instituted to keep them in their places. But both sides agreed that some portion of human existence must remain independent of the sphere of social control. The most eloquent of all defenders of freedom and privacy, Benzamin Constant, who had not forgotten the Jacobin dictatorship, declared that at the very least the liberty of religion, opinion, expression, property, must be guaranteed against arbitrary invasion. We must preserve a minimum area of personal freedom if we are not to 'degrade or deny our nature'. We cannot remain absolutely free. What then must the minimum be? That which a man cannot give up without offending against the essence of his human nature. What is this essence? What are the standards which it entails? This has been and perhaps always will be, a matter of infinite debate. But whatever the principal in terms of which the area of non-interference is to be drawn whether it is that of natural law or natural rights, or the sanctity of the social contact, or any other concept with which men have sought to clarify and justify their convictions, liberty in this sense means liberty from absence of interference beyond the shifting, but always recognisable, frontier. 'The only freedom which deserve the name is that of pursuing our own good in our own way, said the most celebrated of its champions. If this is so its compulsion every justified? Mill had no doubt it was. Since justice demands that all individuals be entitled to a minimum of freedom, all other individuals be were necessity to be restrained, if need be by force, from depriving anyone of it.

All the errors which a man is likely to commit against advice and warning are far outweighed by the evil of allowing others to constrain him to what, they deem is good. The defence of liberty consists in the 'negative' goal of warding off interference. To threaten a man with persecution unless he submits to a life in which he exercises no choices of his goals; to block before him every door but one no matter how noble the prospect upon which it opens or how benevolent the motives of those who arrange this, is to sin against the truth that he is a man, a being with a life of his own to live.

Three facts about this position may be noted. In the first place Mill confuses two distinct notions. One is that all coercion, in so far as it frustrates human desires, bad as such, although it may have to be applied to prevent other, greater evils; while non-interference, which is the opposite of coercion, is good as such, although it is not the only good. This is the 'negative' conception of liberty in its classical form. The other is that men should seek to discover the truth, or to develop a certain type of character of which Mill approved- fearless, original, imaginative, independent, non-conforming to the point of eccentricity, and so on and that truth can be found and such character can be bred, only in conditions of freedom. Both these are liberal views, but they are not identical, and the connection between them is, at best, empirical.

In the second place, the doctrine is comparatively modern. There seems to be scarcely any discussion of individual liberty as a conscious political ideal in the ancient world. The domination of this ideal has been the exception rather than the rule, even in the recent history of the West. The sense of privacy itself of the area of personal relationships as something sacred in its own right, derives from a conception of freedom which for all its religious roots is scarcely older, in its developed state, that renaissance or the reformation.

The third characteristic of this notion of liberty is of greater importance. It is that liberty in this sense is not compatible with some kind of autocracy, or at any rate with the absence of self government. Liberty in this sense is principally concerned with the area of control not with its source.

For the positive sense of liberty comes to light if we try to answer the question not "What am I free to do or be?" but By whom am I ruled? Or who is to say what I am and what I am not to be or do? The connection is a good deal more weak than it seemed to many advocates of both.

The Notion of Positive Freedom

The 'positive' sense of the word 'liberty' derives from the wish on the part of the individual to be his own master. The freedom which consists in being one's own master, and the freedom which consists in not being prevented from choosing as I do by other men may on the face of it, seem concepts at no great logical distance from each other no more than negative and positive ways of saying the same thing. One way of making this clear is in terms of the independent momentum which the initially perhaps quite harmless metaphor of self-mastery acquired. Then the dominant self is identified with reason, my higher nature 'real' or 'ideal' or 'autonomous' self, is contrasted with irrational impulse, uncontrolled, desires, my lower nature my empirical or heteronymous self. Presented as divided by an even larger gap: the real self may be conceived as something wider than the individual, as a social 'whole' of which the individual is an element or aspect: a tribe a race a church, a state, the great society of the living and the dead and the yet unborn. This entity is then identified as being the true self which by imposing its collective, or organic single will upon its unwilling members, achieves its own, and therefore their, higher freedom. The perils of using organic metaphors to justify the coercion of some men by others in order to raise them to a higher level of freedom have often been pointed out. But what gives such plausibility as it has to this kind of language is that we recognise that it is possible and at times justifiable, to coerce men in the name of some goal which they would if they were more enlightened themselves pursue but do not because they are blind or ignorant or corrupt. I (it refers to the collective self here) am then claiming that I know what they truly need better than they know it themselves. What, at most this entails is that they would not resist me if they were rational, and as wise as I, and understood their interests as I do. I may declare that they are actually aiming at what in their ignorant state they consciously resist, because there exists within them a hidden entity- their, latent rational will, or their 'true' purpose and that this entity, although it is believed by all that they overtly feel and do and say is their 'real' self of which the poor empirical self in space and time may know nothing or little and that this inner spirit is the only self that deserves to have its wishes into account whatever be the true goal of man, must be identical with his freedom of will.

References: This chapter has been inspired from Berlin, I. (1958) "Two Concepts of Liberty." In Isaiah Berlin (1969) *Four Essays on Liberty*. Oxford: Oxford University Press and from lectures delivered at Hindu College, University of Delhi.

10

Social Issues and their Proposed Remedies

Women in various parts of the country face such day-to-day problems that perhaps, we cannot even think of while leading our comfortable lives, enhanced by technology!

A. In earlier times, most villages and small towns did not have restrooms at residences, which forced people; inclusive of women and children, to go in the farms and on road-sides to defecate. This resulted in extreme inconvenience and embarrassment, specially for the women along with obvious unsanitary conditions.

However, now the condition of sanitary system is a lot better in India and most houses have in-built restrooms, but there are still some villages which are devoid of this facility. Unfortunately enough, some women still are made to face immense inconvenience and embarrassment by having to defecate in the open. Not only is such a practice extremely unhygienic and unhealthy, but it also puts a lot of mental strain on the women who have to undergo this everyday. This becomes a bigger task when they are menstruating. According to a survey conducted by an esteemed NGO, GOONJ, most women in Rajasthan still use the traditional cloth pad and in times of scarcity even used their old cholis (blouses) as a pad. On interacting with these women, the NGO members realised that their challenges are the same as millions of women across rural and slum India; that of lack of awareness, access and availability of even clean cotton cloth for their basic monthly need. In absence of cotton cloth many spoke about using synthetic cloth. Many have had to travel 50-60 km to the nearest town to buy a piece of flalin fabric to be used as a pad. Some even confessed putting sand between pieces of cloth to absorb the blood. some shared how having no toilets adds to their misery, specially during these days!

Along with educating women about health and sanitation, public restrooms should be constructed in every village and town. Also, people should be made aware and made to realise that they should make sure that their residences have restrooms.

Not only is the government constructing public restrooms to improve the sanitary conditions, but citizens are also assisting the government to our relief. Also, initiatives taken by NGOs such as GOONJ are much appreciated and acknowledged.

Recently, two Muslim girls residing in a small village in the district of Firozabad, refused to get married until their in-laws constructed restrooms in their respective houses and to our surprise the in-laws conceded to what the girls had demanded! We need more such instances and more such citizens to help our nation and our women progress.

B. No matter how much our society has progressed, in some parts of the country the birth of a girl child is still mourned. A girl is still considered a financial burden by some. Their safety and security still gives sleepless nights to many. This attitude encourages child marriage of young girls, keeping them deprived of their childhood, family and most importantly, education.

We need incentive programmes to prevent such practices and more importantly, to change the perception of the society towards females. They should be made to realise that daughters are not a burden! A female only facilitates procreation. Today, girls are as efficient as boys in every possible field, if not more. They should be treated with love and dignity.

Apna Beti, Apna Dhan (ABAD), which translates to "My daughter, My wealth", is one of India's first ***conditional cash transfer*** programmes dedicated to delaying young marriages across the nation. In 1994, the Indian government implemented this programme in the state of Haryana. On the birth of a mother's first, second or third child, they are set to receive Rs 500 or US $ 11 within the first fifteen days to cover their post-delivery needs. Along with this, the government gives Rs 2,500 or US $55, to invest in a long-term savings bond in the daughter's name, which can be later encashed for Rs 25,000 or US $550, after her 18th birthday. She is only entitled to the money if she is not married. Anju Malhotra, an expert on child marriage and adolescent girls, said, "No other conditional cash transfer has this focus of delaying marriage. It's an incentive to encourage parents to value their daughters."[19]

Another such initiative was undertaken by the Uttar Pradesh government, aimed at encouraging girl child education. Under this scheme each girl child, belonging to low income or poverty stricken families, is entitled to receive Rs 30,000 cash along with a laptop, upon clearing the class 12th examination. This initiative has also helped the girl child literacy rate in the state of Uttar Pradesh. However, there are several lacunaes in the exercise of this initiative like many girls only get cash and not laptops. Sometimes only girls who score 90 per cent and above in the 12th examinations are awarded with cash prize and laptops, which is inconsistent with the scheme which requires the state to give cash and laptops to each girl who clears the said examination.

There are similar initiatives launched in various other states like Gujarat, Madhya Pradesh, Tamil Nadu etc.

We need more such initiatives for our educational-socio-economic growth. Education for all is very important. Boys should also be educated because most of the crimes are committed by males who are uneducated and hence, unaware. As Gandhiji once said, "If a boy is educated, a child gets literacy, but if a girl is educated, the whole family gets literacy." That's how vital girl child education is.

C. A very basic obstacle in the growth of women in our country is that they are dependent on their male counterparts for every little thing. They haven't yet gained the freedom and independence to lead their own lives in the way that they'd desire.

For instance, according to a UN Report household chores undertaken by women would contribute almost 20-30 per cent to our GDP. Such chores are a form of disguised and unpaid labour. We are not even a middle income economy! Women are abstained from working outside their homes because they are considered only to play the role of a wife, daughter, sister, mother and the like and hence, expected to stay indoors and look after their families. But one needs to understand that no one sex has been innately assigned a specific role. If such activities undertaken by women are taken into account then that would improve our GDP by almost 20 per cent, which is considerably a huge amount!

One such instance of according independence to women is the story of a small village called Pudukkottai, situated in Tamil Nadu. It is one of India's poorest districts where cycling seemed the chosen medium for rural women. Over 100,000 rural women, most of them neo-literates, took to cycling as a symbol of independence, freedom and mobility. The whole phenomenon was the brainchild of the popular former district collector, Sheela Rani Chunkath. Her idea in 1991 was to train female activists so that literary would reach women in the interior. She also included ***mobility*** as a part of the literacy drive. This flowed from the fact that lack of mobility among women played a significant role in undermining their confidence. Chunkath pushed the banks to grant loans for the women to buy cycles. She also got each block to accept specific duties in promoting the drive. As the top official in the district, she gave it personal attention.

In a single week in 1992, more than 70,000 women displayed their cycling skills at the public 'exhibition-cum-contests' run by Arivoli. An impressed UNICEF sanctioned fifty mopeds for Arivoli women activists.

Cycling in many ways, boosts income. Some of the women there who sold agricultural or other produce within a group of villages, for them, the cycles cut down on time wasted in waiting for buses. This is crucial in poorly connected areas. Further, it enlarges the area one hopes to cover. Of course, it the sense of self-respect and freedom it brings is vital. Those who had cycles could carry out different tasks with nonchalance. One could spot a lady on a cycle in some remote area, with two children sitting on the handle, produce on the carrier and pots water hung on her back, cycling kilometres together to work or home! "The main thing was the confidence it gave women.

Very importantly, it reduced their dependence on men", said N. Kannammal, Arivoli central coordinator and one of the pioneers of the cycling movement. This movement turned out to be a great success in enabling the women to become self-sufficient and independent.

Taking inspiration from this, we must take initiative to start more such programmes.

Sometimes what happens is that rural illiterate women, tend to get economically dependent on their male counterparts and feel that they are unproductive because of them being illiterate. Many take course to agricultural activities, some start working in factories while few become household maids or cooks. Apart from the mentioned activities, cooperative societies could be formed in villages or in each block, encouraging women to take up activities like making hand-woven sweaters, embroidered bedsheets, preparing tiffins for factory or agricultural workers, making pickles etc. These would be paid activities. Such activities would give them a sense of confidence in their innate skills. Basically, it will make them feel proud of themselves by earning money from what they do best!

If we work together as a nation, on the aforementioned proposals and many more such schemes, India would definitely come out a winner in empowering it's women and in turn, empowering the whole country!

Part – II

11

Child Rights in India

Who is a child? This simple question has somewhat complex answers. Most of the world's civilisations did not consider children human beings with full human value. Thus, childhood was not an independent category until the beginning of the eighteenth century. Legislation did not deal with childhood as a period of life that needs special measures or protection until the early nineteenth century. In his book, *L'enfant ET la vie familial sous I'Ancien Regime,* Phillippe Aries said that the child in the Middle Ages did not exist as an independent anthropological category and therefore, children did not need to be taken into consideration.

The law, policy and practice of child welfare have undergone significant changes from a historical point of view. Before 1839, authority and control was important. It was an established common law doctrine that the father had absolute rights over his children. After this, the welfare principle was reflected in the dominant family ideology of the family.

The traditional Indian view of welfare is based on *daya, dana, dakshina, bhiksha, ahimsa, samya-bhava, swadharma* and *tyaga*. It was believed that the wellbeing of children depended on these values. It was only during the twentieth century that the concept of child rights emerged. This shift in focus from the welfare to the rights approach is significant. Rights are entitlements. They also imply obligations and goals. The rights approach is primarily concerned with issues of social justice, non-discrimination, equity and empowerment. The rights perspective is embodied in the ***United Nations Convention on the Rights of the Child (UNCRC), 1989,*** which is a landmark in international human rights legislation. India ratified this convention in December 1992.

The UNCRC defines child rights as the minimum entitlements and freedoms that should be afforded to every citizen below the age of 18 regardless of race, national origin, colour, gender, language, religion, opinions, wealth, birth status, disability or other characteristics. Some children are abandoned. They are left to fend for themselves on the streets. They are deprived of their right to education and health. They are subjected to cruel and inhuman treatment. Therefore, they require rights. These rights ensure freedom of children and civil rights.

The UNCRC outlines the fundamental human rights that should be afforded to children in four broad categories that cover all civil, political, social, economic and cultural rights of every child. These rights are as follows:-

1. **Right to Survival**
   - Right to be born
   - Right to minimum standards of food, shelter and clothing
   - Right to live with dignity
   - Right to healthcare, to safe drinking water, nutritious food, a clean and safe environment, and information to help them stay healthy.
2. **Right to Protection**
   - Right to be protected from all sorts of violence
   - Right to be protected from neglect
   - Right to be protected from physical and sexual abuse
   - Right to be protected from dangerous drugs.
3. **Right to Participation**
   - Right to freedom of opinion
   - Right to freedom of expression
   - Right to freedom of association
   - Right to information

- Right to participate in any decision-making that involves them directly or indirectly.

4. **Right to Development**
   - Right to education
   - Right to learn
   - Right to relax and play
   - Right to all forms of development- emotional, mental and physical.

The Indian Constitution accords rights children as citizens of the country and in keeping with their special status the State has even enacted special laws. The Constitution encompasses most rights included in the UNCRC as Fundamental Rights and Directive Principles of State Policy. The Directive Principles of State Policy articulate social and economic rights that have been declared to be "fundamental in the governance of the country and... the duty of the State to apply…in making laws" (Article 37). The government has the flexibility to undertake appropriate legislative and administrative measure to ensure child rights. These directives have enabled the judiciary to deliver some landmark judgements promoting child rights, leading to Constitutional Amendments such as the 86th Amendment to the Constitution that made Right to Education a fundamental right.

Constitutional guarantees that are meant specifically for children include:

- Right to elementary education for all children in the age group of 6-14 years. (***Article 21 A***)
- Right to be protected from hazardous employment till the age of 14 years. ***(Article 24***)
- Right to be protected from abuse and forced by economic necessity to enter occupations unsuited to their age or strength. (***Article 39 (e))***
- Right to equal opportunity to facilities to develop in a healthy manner and in conditions of freedom and dignity and guaranteed protection of childhood and youth against moral and material abandonment. (***Article 39 (f))***

- Right to early childhood education to all children until they complete the age of six years. (***Article 45***)

Besides the aforementioned rights, children also have rights as an equal citizen of India, just as any other adult male of female:

- Right to equality. ***(Article 14)***
- Right against discrimination. ***(Article 15)***
- Right to life and personal liberty. ***(Article 21)***
- Right of being protected from being trafficked and forced into bonded labour. ***(Article 23)***
- Right of minorities for protection of their interests. ***(Article 29)***
- Right of weaker section people to be protected from social injustice and all forms of exploitation. ***(Article 46)***
- Right to nutrition and standard of living and improved public health. ***(Article 47)***

But Do All Children Get These Rights?

Out of every 1000 children born in India, 31 die before they are one year old. In contrast to this, in Japan and Singapore, only two or three out of 1000 children die before they turn one year old. Further, for every 1000 men in India, there are only 933 women. Isn't that appalling?

Most children in India who do get a chance to go to school, go to government-run schools which are often filthy, where the quality of education and teaching is poor, sometimes they are not even provided with books or toys or learning aids and where they are not treated with respect. Only a very small percentage of children go to good schools where they are cared for and taught well.

What is education? Is it a means to achieve an end or is it an end in itself? Most importantly, is this so called "fundamental right" available to all or is it just availed by the affluent few?! The answers to these questions are rather complex and extremely diverse.

It is the moral responsibility of the global community to facilitate the 'tools of growth and empowerment' to those who do not have access to them. Education is the greatest tool for empowerment and in delivering education, the policy-makers should ensure to empower both the socially and economically underprivileged class.

The United Nations Convention on the Rights of the Child (UNCRC), 1989, is a landmark legislation in the sphere of international human rights. The UNCRC guarantees **Right to education** to every child across the world, as a **fundamental right**, under the broad head of Right to Development.

For instance, Article 21A of the Indian Constitution, encompasses the right of children aged between 6 to 14 years to obtain free and compulsory education. The rationale behind this is obviously to deliver education to children belonging to the poor section of the society, thus, improving the literacy rate. It hasn't, however, ameliorated the situation much. Forty million children in India work as child labourers, never going to school and having no chance to develop. Most children who do get a chance to attend school, go to government-run schools which are more often than not, ill-administered and this is the situation in a country like India which is still relatively developed than other nations. The condition of such underprivileged children is even worse in underdeveloped countries like Africa.

However, the reservation or affirmative action policy for the scheduled castes and scheduled tribes in India, has been able to accelerate the literacy rates overtime. From 1999 to 2012 there has been a considerable reduction of illiteracy by 23 per cent, among the scheduled castes. For higher education, there is still a glass ceiling, which will take time to breakthrough. This explains why there is a decline of SC/ST population working as 'main workers' and a corresponding increase in the said population as 'marginal workers'.

Thus, the policy-makers need to remember that it is not only necessary to increase the net education but also to increase it in a manner that the vertical growth of education empowers them to establish themselves as mainstream contributors of the society.

Another important aspect in this context which needs to be taken into consideration is : what actually is the goal of education? Is it just to secure good jobs, seek achievement in life or to learn and attain knowledge?

If we wish for a better future and world peace, we should concentrate on imparting quality education to each and every citizen of this world. We should make students content-focused rather than achievement-focused. It is often seen that assessing a student's aptitude by way of examination grades, encourages rote learning and cramming among children. Our environment is still polluted and our earth still remains in danger, despite the growth of the world economy! It is often seen that even highly qualified people litter their surroundings unabashedly, use their personal vehicles instead of public transport, thereby, increasing. The reason being that our current education system tutors children to compete and seek well-paid jobs rather than enhancing their intellectual capacities.

The global community should come together to democratise education by pouring in strategic thinking and physical as well as financial resources to those sections of the society that have been left undeserved. It would be erroneous to think that those who are privileged can by itself liberate the depressed sections of the society, but what can be done on a global front is, to empower these underprivileged groups to liberate themselves on their own. The only tool to achieve such an aim is education.

From 2004 to 2012, the number of households without a literate member have decreased across all social groups in both rural and urban India. The decrease is significantly more for scheduled groups as compared to the rest. Hence, the affirmative policy does help improve the education standards.

Despite improving numbers, there is still much to be done to bring education of the socially underprivileged on par with the general population. According to the National Sample Survey, the SC and ST groups have a higher proportion of persons at low levels of consumption than the general population in every state. It can be observed that in 2009-10, the All India rural poverty ratio was 33.8 while that of the Scheduled Castes was 42.2, a clear indicator of acute poverty of the Scheduled Castes in our country. So we need to take into consideration both kinds of children, i.e., the economically backward classes as well as the socially backward classes.

The solution is not to give a man a fish (read **liberty**), and feed him for a day; it is rather to teach a man to fish, and you feed **(liberate)** him for a lifetime.

Furthermore, most children have never had a chance to be heard. Their opinions regarding their city, their school, their environment, is never asked for or never taken into consideration by adults. Then how can we say they have a right to freedom of speech and expression?

Unfortunately enough, thousands of children each year are bought or kidnapped by agents from poor rural areas, and sold as domestic workers or exploited in many other ways. Children are sometimes abused by adults within their own families. Therefore, not all children are safe.

However, many legal mechanisms have been created to ensure that each child gets their due rights. Few of these mechanisms are as follows:-

1. Various organisations, such as the following, have also been formed to protect and empower women and children, under the supervision of the ***Ministry of Women and Child Development***:-

- **A.** National Institute of Public Cooperation and Child Development
- **B.** National Commission for Women
- **C.** Rashtriya Mahila Kosh
- **D.** National Commission for Protection of Child Rights
- **E.** Central Adoption Resource Agency
- **F.** Central Social Welfare Board

The broad mandate of the Ministry is to have holistic development of Women and Children. It formulates plans, policies and programmes; enacts/ amends legislations, guides and coordinates the efforts of both governmental as well as non-governmental organisations working in the field of women and child development. Besides this, the Ministry implements certain innovative programmes for women and children. These programmes cover welfare and support services, training for employment and income generation, awareness generation and gender sensitisation. These programmes play a complimentary role to the other general developmental programmes in the sectors of health, education, rural development etc. All these efforts are directed to ensure that women are empowered both economically and socially, thus, become equal partners in national development along with men.

2. National Commission for Protection of Child Rights- The National Commission for Protection of Child Rights (NCPCR) was set up in March 2007 under the Commission for Protection of Child Rights Act, 2005, an Act of Parliament (December 2005). The Commission's mandate is to ensure that all laws, policies, programmes, and administrative mechanisms are in consonance with the child rights perspective as enshrined in the Constitution of India and also the UN Convention on the Rights of the Child. A Child is defined as a person below the age of 18 years.

The Commission visualises a rights-based perspective flowing into national policies and programmes, along with nuanced responses at the state, district and block levels, taking care of specifications and strengths of each region. In order to cover every child, it seeks a deeper penetration into communities and households, and expects that the ground experiences gathered at the field are taken into consideration by all the authorities at the higher level. Thus, the Commission sees an indispensable role for the state, sound institution building processes, respect for decentralisation at the local bodies and community level and larger social concern for children and their well-being.

3. UNICEF- The United Nation's Children's Emergency Fund (UNICEF) is a United Nations programme headquartered in New York City that provides long-term humanitarian and developmental assistance to children and mothers in developing countries. It was created by the United Nations General Assembly on December 11, 1946, to provide emergency food and healthcare to children in countries that been devastated by World War II.

UNICEF is on the ground in over 150 countries and territories to help children survive and thrive, from early childhood through adolescence. The world's largest provider of vaccines for developing countries, UNICEF supports child health and nutrition, good water and sanitation, quality basic education for all boys and girls, and the protection of children from violence, exploitation and AIDS. UNICEF is funded entirely by the voluntary contributions of individuals, businesses, foundations and governments.

Our legislature has been proactive in forming various acts to protect child rights. However, these acts/ rights are also not free from lacunae.

Rights and Remedies

1. *Right to Education:*
   Vidya dadati vinayam,
   Vinaya dadati paatrataam,
   paatratva dhanamaapnoti,
   dhanaat dharmam tatatsukham.

This translates into: Education gives Humility, Humility gives Character, from character one gets wealth, from wealth one gets righteousness, in righteousness there is joy.

This sloka clearly explains the importance of education in one's life. Our Constitution makers acknowledged the vitality of education and therefore, education is a fundamental right in India.

Article 45 of the Constitution guarantees Right to early childhood education to all children until they complete the age of six years. Further, Article 21A, inserted into the Constitution after the 86th Amendment, encompasses the right of children aged between 6 to 14 years to obtain free and compulsory education. The rationale behind this is obviously to deliver education to children belonging to the poor section of the society, thus, improving the literacy rate. It hasn't, however, ameliorated the situation much.

Literacy and level of education are basic indicators of the level of development achieved by the society.

Literacy rate of India in 2011 was 74.04 per cent. The Male literacy rate is 82.14 per cent and Female literacy rate is 65.46 per cent according to Census 2011. Among the Indian states, **Kerala has the highest literacy rate 93.91 per cent** and then Mizoram, 91.58 per cent.

Among the Union Territories, **Lakshadweep has the highest literacy rate of 92.28 per cent.**

Bihar has the lowest literacy rate in India with 63.82 per cent. The Male literacy is highest in Lakshadweep 96.11 per cent and Kerala 96.02 per cent.

The Female literacy is highest in Kerala 91.98 per cent and Mizoram 89.40 per cent.

Lowest male literacy is in Bihar 73.39 per cent. Lowest female literacy is in Rajasthan 52.66 per cent.

Literacy rate in rural areas was 71 per cent in 2014, compared to 86 per cent in urban areas, while among the age group of seven years and above, male literacy rate was found higher than the female literacy rate, according to NSSO survey released recently.

Among the age group of seven year and above, the male literacy rate was pegged at 83 per cent vis-à-vis the female literacy rate of 67 per cent.

Similarly, it was found in the rural areas, nearly 4.5 per cent of males and 2.2 per cent of females completed education level of graduation and above, while in urban areas 17 per cent of males and 13 per cent of females completed this level of education. The details are part of a survey on 'Social Consumption: Education' during the National Sample Survey (NSS) 71st Round, January to June 2014, conducted by the National Sample Survey Organisation (NSSO) under the Ministry of Statistics and Programme Implementation. The survey covered entire country with samples taken from 36,479 households in rural areas and 29,447 in urban areas from 4,577 villages and 3,720 urban blocks.

According to its findings, literacy rate among age group of seven years and above in the country was 75 per cent. In rural areas, it was 71 per cent compared to 86 per cent in urban areas.

Adult literacy (age 15 years and above) rate in India was around 71 per cent. For adults also, literacy rate in rural areas was lower than that in urban areas. In rural areas, adult literacy rate was 64 per cent compared to 84 per cent in urban areas.

"No significant difference between rural and urban India existed in terms of distance for physical access to primary schooling. In both rural and urban areas, nearly 99 per cent households reported availability of primary school within 2 kms from the house," the survey said.

For accessing educational institutions providing higher level of learning, say upper primary or secondary, a lower proportion of households in rural areas compared to that in urban areas reported existence of such facilities within 2 kms, it added.

Nearly 86 per cent of rural households and 96 per cent of urban households reported upper primary schools within a distance of 2 kms from the house while nearly 60 per cent of rural households and 91 per cent of urban households reported secondary schools at such a distance, it revealed.

The proportion of persons having completed higher level of education, say, graduation and above, was more in the urban areas than in the rural areas.

In the rural areas, nearly 4.5 per cent of males and 2.2 per cent of females completed education level of graduation and above, while in the urban areas 17 per cent of males and 13 per cent of females completed this level of education.

In rural areas, majority of the students were attending government institutions predominantly up to higher secondary levels, whereas a completely different picture was observed in urban areas.

In rural areas, 72 per cent of the students at primary level, 76 per cent at upper primary level and 64 per cent at secondary and higher secondary level attended government institutions, the survey said.

At primary level, expenditure per student in urban areas was Rs 10,083, more than four times than that in rural areas, pegged at Rs 2,811.

Average expenditure on technical education in private aided and unaided institutions varied between nearly 1.5-2.5 times of that in government institutions.

Nearly 46 per cent of expenditure for general education and 73 per cent of the expenditure for technical education was on course fee.

For students pursuing general courses, 15 per cent was spent on private coaching as against 3 per cent for students pursuing technical/ professional education (including vocational).

Nearly 6 per cent of rural households and 29 per cent of urban household possessed computer. Among households in the country, with at least one member aged above 14 years and above, nearly 27 per cent had internet access in the survey year, 2014.

The proportions were 16 per cent among rural households and 49 per cent of urban households, the survey said.

Among persons of age while in urban areas, 31 per cent at primary level, 38 per cent at upper primary level as well as secondary and higher secondary level, attended government institutions.

Average expenditure per student incurred and/or to be incurred during the current academic session was nearly Rs 6,788 for general education, Rs 62,841 for technical/ professional (except vocational) and Rs 27,676 for 14-29 years, nearly 18 per cent in rural areas and 49 per cent in urban areas were able to operate a computer in the age group of 14-29 years.

The overall literacy rate in the country may have gone up to 74.4 per cent, but the drop in the illiteracy rate has not matched the increase in population.

Between 2001 and 2011, the population above the age of 7 grew by 18.65 crore but the decrease in the number of illiterates is just 3.11 crore.

A 2015 UNESCO report read that in terms of absolute numbers, India - with 28.7 crore illiterates - was the country with the largest number of adults without basic literacy skills in 2010-11 compared to 2000-01 when it had 30.4 crore illiterates.

The fact that illiteracy is not being dealt with is explicit from the enrollment rates in primary and upper primary schools. Over 12 years

(2000-01 to 2013-14), the number of children who enrolled in primary schools increased by just 1.86 crore, and at the upper primary level by just over 2 crore. The population during this period, however, increased by more than 18 crore.

"Over the past few years, there has been a dip in the enrollment rate across the country compared to the growth in population," says A S Seetharamu, a former professor of the Institute of Social and Economic Change.

Going by 2011 Census data, most states, barring a few like Nagaland, have recorded an increase in population but the enrollment rate does not reflect that.

The country also seems to be having a problem with retaining people in schools and colleges. An average of 326 out of 1,000 students in rural areas are dropping out, while the same is 383 per 1,000 in urban areas, the National Sample Survey Organisation's (NSSO) last survey reveals. This data counts people up to the age of 29.

UNESCO has put the number of out-of-school (OOS) children at 17 lakh in India. A survey commissioned by the Centre put the number for 2014 at 61 lakh, with SC and ST children making up 49.03 per cent (29.73 lakh) of these.[20]

One of the reasons behind this problem is that our Constitution guarantees free and compulsory education only up to the age of 14 years and not beyond that. Is such level of education sufficient to make a person completely literate and educated? Is it enough to make a person self-reliant? Indeed no!

We need to make education compulsory for all children up to the age of 18 years so that each child gets the opportunity to at least complete his/her schooling. For instance, in the United States of America, all states require students to attend school until they are between 16 and 18.

Compulsory education laws keep students in school until they are near graduation. Research from the Bureau of Labour Statistics shows there is a direct correlation between the level of education students achieve and their economic future. Those with more education typically make more money and have lower unemployment rates. In 2012, the unemployment rate for workers without a high school diploma was over 12 per cent, while those with at least a diploma had rates of around 8 per cent. On an average, high school graduates make about $9,400 less a year.

Forcing children to attend school does nothing to address the real reasons they decide to drop out. According to BoostUp.org, the top reasons that students quit school include that it was not interesting, they had low family expectations that led to poor attendance and grades or they became teen parents. Perhaps instead of forcing students to sit in a classroom, energy and resources could be used to create schools with relevant, interesting coursework and address some of the social issues that lead to high drop-out numbers.

To assist in reducing the number of drop-outs, we should subsidize education, like Sweden. **Sweden**, pays its students $ 187 (INR 12,472) per month to attend high school! Education is subsidized and the state actually pays parents for child support so that their education can go on without financial obstacles. Such a step would encourage parents to send their children to school and would enable them to complete their high school education(if not further), hence, bringing down the figure of school drop-outs!

It was interestingly pointed out and observed in the landmark case of **T.M.A. Pai Foundation vs. State of Karnataka**[21] that some educational institutions collect, in advance, the fees for the entire course, i.e., for all the years. It was submitted that this was done because the institute was not sure whether the student would leave the institute midstream. It was submitted that if the student left the course midstream then for the remaining years the seat would lie vacant and the institute would suffer. In response to this, the court observed that in its view an educational institution can only charge prescribed fees for one semester/year. If an institution feels that any particular student may leave in midstream then, at the highest, it may require that student to give a bond/bank guarantee that the balance fees for the whole course would be received by the institute even if the student left in midstream. If any educational institution has collected fees in advance, only the fees of that semester/ year can be used by the institution. The balance fees must be kept invested in fixed deposits in a nationalised bank. As and when fees fall due for a semester/year only the fees falling due for that semester/year can be withdrawn by the institution. The rest must continue to remain deposited till such time that they fall due. At the end of the course the interest earned on these deposits must be paid to the student from whom the fees were collected in advance.

Keeping in mind, the ratio laid down by the Hon'ble Supreme Court of India in the said judgment, each student must get the interest earned on the security money paid by them and deposited by schools. If such practice is brought into existence it might help in the acceleration of literacy rates!

- Most parents don't send their children to school because they would rather have their children aid the family income by doing some sort of labour instead of spending money on their education. This is again one of the major reasons for increasing school drop-outs. This happens even when a child has a fundamental right under **Article 39 (e)** to be protected from abuse and forced by economic necessity to enter occupations unsuited to their age or strength.

It is unfortunate that education is seen as a means to achieve an end rather than as an end in itself. It is seen as a pre-requisite to acquire well paid jobs. The economically underprivileged class (in particular) often abstain from education because they feel that they would have to spend on their child's education for so many years which would in turn, put more financial pressure on the family. However, if the proposition laid down in the **T.M.A. Pai Foundation** case is brought to light and made a rule to be followed mandatorily by all educational institutions, it may act as an incentive for such people to send their children to school. If people realise that not only will their child be able to acquire a well paid job or start earning by setting up their own business after acquiring education but also, they would get money in the form of interest secured on their security deposits, they would perhaps look at education as an investment and willingly send their children to school. For many, education would then become an end in itself in some manner. The economically and socially underprivileged class would feel that their expenditure on their child's education is an investment fetching good returns not only after the completion of education in the form of jobs but also on the very point of completion of education. The longer the child studies, the more interest they'd earn on the security deposit. Keeping this psychology into perspective, people can be encouraged to send their children to schools which would in turn accelerate the literacy rates, hence, aiding progress of the whole nation.

One Laptop Per Child

Children are the most important and precious natural resource of any country. Most of the children in the developing world are inadequately educated, or receive no education at all. One in three does not complete the fifth grade.The individual and societal consequences of this chronic global crisis are extremely grave. Children resign their fates to poverty and isolation—just like their parents—never knowing what the light of learning could mean in their lives. At the same time, their governments struggle to compete in a rapidly evolving, global information economy, because it lacks the tools to do so.

Given the resources that developing countries can reasonably allocate to education—sometimes less than $20 per year per person, compared to the approximately $7500 per person spent annually in the U.S.—even a doubled or redoubled national commitment to traditional education, augmented by external and private funding, would not get the job done. Moreover, experience strongly suggests that an incremental increase of "more of the same"—building schools, hiring teachers, buying books and equipment—is a laudable but insufficient response to the problem of bringing true learning possibilities to the vast numbers of children in the developing world.

In 2002, MIT Professor Nicholas Negroponte experienced first-hand how connected laptops transformed the lives of children and their families in a remote Cambodian village. A seed was planted: If every child in the world had access to a computer, what potential could be unlocked? What problems could be solved? These questions eventually led to the foundation of One Laptop per Child, and the creation of the XO laptop.

At the 2006 World Economic Forum in Davos, Switzerland and the United Nations Development Programme (UNDP) announced it support and back the laptop. UNDP released a statement saying they would work with OLPC to deliver "technology and resources to targeted schools in the least developed countries".

In the first years of the project, the Association managed development and logistics, and the Foundation managed fund-raising such as the Give One Get One campaign ("G1G1").

One Laptop Per Child (OLPC) is a non-profit initiative established with the goal of transforming education for children in low-income economies. This goal was to be achieved by creating and distributing educational devices for the developing world, and by creating software and content for those devices.

Its primary goal was transformation of education, by enabling children in low-income countries to have access to content, media and computer-programming environments. At the time that the programme launched, the typical retail price for a laptop was considerably in excess of $1,000 (US), so it was not really feasible to achieve this objective without also bringing a low-cost machine to production. This became the OLPC XO, a low-cost and low-power laptop computer. The project was originally funded by member organisations such as AMD, eBay, Google, Marvell Technology Group, News Corporation, Nortel, Chi Mei Corporation, Red Hat, and Quanta backed in-kind.

The mission of the non-profit organisation lay emphasis on something broader, bigger — One Laptop per Child meant empowerment, engagement, and education:

We aim to provide each child with a rugged, low-cost, low-power, connected laptop. To this end, we have designed hardware, content and software for collaborative, joyful, and self-empowered learning. With access to this type of tool, children are engaged in their own education, and learn, share, and create together. They become connected to each other, to the world and to a brighter future.

The laptops are sold to governments, to be distributed through the ministries of education with the goal of distributing "one laptop per child". The laptops are given to students, similar to school uniforms and ultimately remain the property of the child. The operating system and software is localised to adapt to the languages of the participating countries.

India's Ministry of Human Resource Development, rejected the initiative, in June 2006, saying "it would be impossible to justify an expenditure of this scale on a debatable scheme when public funds continue to be in inadequate supply for well-established needs listed in different policy documents". Later they stated plans to make laptops at $10 each for school children. Two designs submitted to the Ministry from a final year engineering student of Vellore Institute of Technology and a researcher from the Indian Institute of Science, Bangalore in May 2007, allegedly, describe a laptop that could be produced for "$47 per laptop" for even small volumes. The Ministry announced in July 2008 that the cost of their proposed "$10 laptop" would in fact be $100 by the time the laptop became available. In 2010, a related $35 Sakshat Tablet was introduced in India, released the next year as the "Aakash". In 2011, one Aakash was sold for approximately $44 by an Indian company, Data Wind. It intends to launch similar projects in Brazil, Egypt, Panama, Thailand and Turkey. OLPC later expressed support for the initiative.

In 2009, a number of states announced plans to order OLPCs. However, as of 2010, only the State of Manipur had deployed 1000 laptops against an order of 70,000 because OLPC could not meet the conditions of dealing with the government such as offering bank guarantee against any advances, letters of credit in Indian Rupees rather than USD etc.

The OLPC project has been the subject of both extreme appreciation and criticism. It was praised for enabling low-cost, low-power machines; for assuring consensus at ministerial level in many countries that computer literacy is a mainstream part of education; for creating interfaces that worked without literacy in any language, and particularly without literacy in English. It has received criticism specific to its mission, and criticism such as support, ease-of-use, security, content-filtering and privacy issues. Officials in some countries have criticised the project for its suitability and aptness in terms of price, cultural emphasis and priority as compared to other basic needs of people in third-world settings.

"Today, the OLPC initiative is often cited by critics as a failure. However, instead of dismissing the laptops as disappointments, it is important to examine the cause of their decline. This understanding can prevent impediments in the future when trying to implement some other form of information and communication technology in developing nations. Careful analysis about the culture and necessities of the children needs to be done in the countries before shipping the laptops. Laptops need to be customised to local traditions and customs, so that they are appropriate in their new context. Despite its initial setback, the OLPC initiative can improve its success rate by letting go of its Western ideals and adapting its laptops to the appropriate needs of the children who are using them in the developing countries.

The actual distribution of the laptops points to an obvious failure of the programme. When OLPC was first founded, it only took orders in lots of one million. However, no developing nation could risk the capital necessary to buy these one million laptops, especially if there was no data proving the benefits of the programme. OLPC was then forced to lower the minimum purchase number to 250,000 laptops.[3] The founders initially thought that a lot of countries would be willing to pay for these laptops en masse, which would ensure cheaper production costs for individual laptops. However, the target nations do not have that much money; therefore, the minimum deployment size had to be lowered over time. As a result of such unrealistic goals, delivery of the laptops was low. Figure 1 shows the actual number of laptops distributed in specific countries by the OLPC foundation. The first number is the data shown on OLPC's main website, and the second number is the actual number of laptops in the various schools. A major cause of discrepancy between the two numbers is that the OLPC website does not distinguish between ordered, shipped, or delivered laptops. Even then, the actual numbers are low, and the global distribution is sparse. Out of the machines that were delivered to the various schools, it is not safe to assume that they are all actually being used by the children. In Uruguay, "27.4 per cent of machines were out of commission in a recent poll, or more than 100,000 out of the 400,000 in the country."[4] Of the laptops deployed within Uruguay, one in every four laptops was not used by the schools because of malfunctioning and lack of technical support. This issue further reduces the number of active laptops within the OLPC project and amplifies the failure of the project. Similar numbers would also be found in other countries; however, no research has been done yet to support this claim. The evidence clearly suggests that the OLPC project fell significantly short of its initial goals of providing millions of children with its XO laptops".[22]

2. Child Labour

Child labour is the practice of having children engaged in economic activity, on part- or full-time basis. This practice deprives children of their childhood, and is also, harmful to their physical and mental development. Poverty, lack of good schools and growth of informal economy are considered as the major causes of and behind the malpractice of child labour in India. The 1998 national Census of India estimated the total number of child labour, aged 4–15, to be at 12.6 million, out of a total child population of 253 million in 5–14 age group.

A 2009–10 nationwide survey found child labour prevalence had reduced to 4.98 million children (or less than two per cent of children in 5–14 age group). The 2011 national census of India found the total number of child labour, aged 5–14, to be at 4.35 million, and the total child population to be 259.64 million in that age group. The child labour problem is not unique to India; worldwide, about 217 million children work, many full-time.

Indian law specifically defines 64 industries as hazardous and it is a criminal offence to employ children in such hazardous industries. In 2001, an estimated one per cent of all child workers, or about 120,000 children in India were in a hazardous job. Notably, Constitution of India prohibits child labour in hazardous industries (but not in non-hazardous industries) as a Fundamental Right under Article 24. According to studies conducted by the UNICEF India with its large population, has the highest number of labourers in the world who are under 14 years of age, while sub-Saharan African countries have the highest percentage of children who are deployed as child labour. International Labour Organisation estimates that agriculture at 60 per cent is the largest employer of child labour in the world, while United Nation's Food and Agriculture Organisation estimates 70 per cent of child labour is indulged in agriculture and related activities. Apart from agriculture, child labour can be seen in almost all informal sectors of the Indian economy.

In December 2014, the U.S. Department of Labour issued a list of goods produced by child labour or forced labour, wherein, India sadly figured among 74 countries where significant incidence of critical working conditions has been observed. Unlike any other country, India was attributed 23 goods, the majority of which are produced by child labourers in the manufacturing sector.

Article 24 of India's Constitution prohibits **hazardous** child labour. Additionally, various laws and the Indian Penal Code, such as the Juvenile Justice (care and protection) of Children Act-2000, and the Child Labour (Prohibition and Abolition) Act-1986 provide a basis in law to identify, prosecute and stop child labour in India.

Some child rights activists argue that child labour must include every child who is not in school because he or she is a hidden child worker. UNICEF, however, points out that India faces major shortages of schools, classrooms and teachers particularly in rural areas where 90 per cent of child labour problem is observed. About one in five primary schools have just one teacher to teach students across all grades.

After its independence from colonial rule, India has passed a number of constitutional protections and laws on child labour. The Constitution of India in the Fundamental Rights and the Directive Principles of State Policy prohibits child labour below the age of 14 years in any factory or mine or castle or engaged in any other hazardous employment (Article 24). The constitution also envisioned that India shall, by 1960, provide infrastructure and resources for free and compulsory education to all children of the age six to 14 years. (Article 21-A and Article 45).

India has a federal form of government, and labour being a subject in the Concurrent List, both the central and state governments can and have legislated on child labour. The major national legislative developments include the following:

The Factories Act of 1948: The Act prohibits the employment of children below the age of 14 years in any factory. The law also placed rules on who, when and how long can pre-adults aged 15–18 years be employed in any factory.

The Mines Act of 1952: The Act prohibits the employment of children below 18 years of age in a mine.

The Child Labour (Prohibition and Regulation) Act of 1986: The Act prohibits the employment of children below the age of 14 years in hazardous occupations identified in a list by the law. The list was expanded in 2006, and again in 2008.

The Juvenile Justice (Care and Protection) of Children Act of 2000: This law made it a crime, punishable with a prison term, for anyone to procure or employ a child in any hazardous employment or in bondage.

The Right of Children to Free and Compulsory Education Act of 2009: The law mandates free and compulsory education to all children aged 6 to 14 years. This legislation also mandated that 25 per cent of seats in every private school must be allocated for children from disadvantaged groups and physically challenged children.

India formulated a National Policy on Child Labour in 1987. This Policy seeks to adopt a gradual and sequential approach with a focus on rehabilitation of children working in hazardous occupations. It envisioned strict enforcement of Indian laws on child labour combined with development programmes to address the root causes of child labour such as poverty. In 1988, this led to the National Child Labour Project (NCLP) initiative. This legal and development initiative continues, with a current central government funding of Rs 6 billion, targeted solely to eliminate child labour in India. Despite these efforts, child labour remains a major challenge for India. No child below age of 14 years shall be employed to work in any factory or mine or engaged in any hazardous employment.

The original child labour law banned employment of children below 14 in only 18 hazardous industries. The amendments also make it clear that children between 14 and 18 years will also not be allowed to work in hazardous industries. The changes in the labour law also provide for stricter punishment for employers for violation. While there is no penalty provision for parents for the first offence, the employer would be liable for punishment even for the first violation.

What counts as work, per say, depends on specific social circumstances and activities along with their interpretation. Emily Durkheim defined work through three principles in the context of the Industrial Revolution, wherein the society moved from simple to complex structures. For him, work determines division of labour where social needs are to be satisfied.

Secondly, the causes and conditions of work are co-dependent. And the third principle discusses the classificatory principles presenting abnormal forms. Labour as an occupational category of human activity started with a different equation as opposed to the matrix of market formations subsequently, especially the current society which shows that these activities are not simply its survival strategies, but are for the creation of surplus and its exploitation.[23] This rational principle leads the concept of child labour.

India is sadly the home to the largest number of child labourers in the world. The census found an increase in the number of child labourers from 11.28 million in 1991 to 12.59 million in 2001. M.V. Foundation in Andhra Pradesh found nearly 400,000 children, mostly girls between seven and 14 years of age, toiling for 14-16 hours a day in cotton seed production across the country of which 90 per cent are employed in Andhra Pradesh. Forty per cent of the labour in a precious stone cutting sector is children. NGOs have discovered the use of child labourers in mining industry in Bellary District in Karnataka in spite of a harsh ban on the same. In urban areas there is a high employment of children in the zari and embroidery industry.

Poverty and lack of social security are the main causes of child labour. The increasing gap between the rich and the poor, privatisation of basic services and the neo-liberal economic policies are causes major sections of the population out of employment and without basic needs. This adversely affects children more than any other group. Entry of multi-national corporations into industry without proper mechanisms to hold them accountable has lead to the use of child labour. Lack of quality universal education has also contributed to children dropping out of school and entering the labour force. A major concern is that the actual number of child labourers goes undetected. Laws that are meant to protect children from hazardous labour are not very effective and often not implemented as they should be.

A growing occurence is using children as domestic workers in urban areas. The conditions in which children work are extremely unregulated and they are often made to work without food, and very low wages, resembling situations of slavery. There are cases of physical, sexual and emotional abuse of child domestic workers. The argument mostly advanced for domestic work is that families have placed their children in these homes for care and employment. There has been a recent notification by the Ministry of Labour making child domestic work as well as employment of children in dhabas, tea stalls and restaurants "hazardous" occupations.

According to HAQ: Centre For Child Rights, child labour is highest among schedules tribes, Muslims, schedule castes and OBC children. The persistence of child labour is due to the inefficiency of the law, administrative system and because it benefits employers who can reduce general wage levels. HAQ argues that distinguishing between hazardous and non-hazardous employment is counter-productive to the elimination of child labour. Various growing concerns have pushed children out of school and into employment such as forced displacement due to development projects, Special Economic Zones; loss of jobs of parents in a slowdown, farmers' suicide; armed conflict and high costs of health care. Girl children are often used in domestic labour within their own homes. There is lacunae in our laws and also the administration to enable the complete ban of child labour.

Bonded child labour is a latent phenomenon, as a majority of them are found in the informal sector. Bonded labour means the employment of a person against a loan or debt or social obligation by the family of the child or the family as a whole. It is a form of slavery. Children who are bonded with their family or inherit a debt from their parents are often found in agricultural sector or assisting their families in brick kilns, and stone quarries. Individual pledging of children is unfortunately a growing phenomenon these days that usually leads to trafficking of children to urban areas for employment and have children working in small production houses versus factories. Bonded labourers in India are mostly migrant workers, which opens them up to more exploitation. Also they mostly come from low caste groups such as dalits or marginalised tribal groups. Bonded child labourers stand a very high risk to physical and sexual abuse and neglect sometimes leading to death. They often are psychologically and mentally disturbed and do not get to learn much social or survival skills.

In 2000, the ILO estimated that 5.5 million children had been forced in labour in Asia, while the Bonded Labour Liberation Front placed 10 million bonded children in India alone. In 1998, the Government of India tagged bonded child labour as a marginal problem with only 3000 or such cases. A survey in Tamil Nadu in 1995 discovered 125,000 bonded child labourers in the state alone. Child bonded labour in India is mostly in the agricultural sector but has in recent times been moving into other sectors as well such as beedi-rolling, brick kilns, carpet weaving, commercial sexual exploitation, construction, fireworks and matches factories, hotels, hybrid cottonseed production, leather, mines, quarries, silk, synthetic gems, etc.

The presence of a large number of child labourers is regarded as a serious issue in terms of economic welfare. Children who work fail to get the necessary education. They do not get the opportunity to develop physically, intellectually, emotionally and psychologically. In terms of the physical condition of children, children are not ready for long monotonous and tiring work because they become exhausted easier and quicker than adults. This reduces their physical conditions and makes the children more vulnerable to disease.

Children in hazardous working conditions are even in worse condition. Children who work, instead of going to school, remain illiterate which limits their ability to contribute to their own well being as well as to the community they live in. Child labour, certainly, has long-term adverse effects for India.

To keep an economy prospering, an important factor is to have an educated workforce equipped with relevant skills for the needs of the industries. The young hands today, will form India's human capital tomorrow. Child labour undoubtedly results in a trade-off with human capital accumulation.

Child labour in India are employed majorly (70 per cent) in the agricultural sector, some in low-skilled labour-intensive sectors such as sari weaving or as domestic helpers, which require neither formal education nor training, but some in heavy industry such as coal mining.

According to the International Labour Organisation (ILO), there are tremendous economic benefits for developing nations by sending children to school instead of work. Without education, children do not gain the necessary skills such as English literacy and technical aptitude that will increase their productivity to enable them to secure higher-skilled jobs in future with higher wages that will lift them out of poverty.

Many NGOs like Bachpan Bachao Andolan, Childfund Care India, Talaash Association, Child Rights and You, Global March against child labour, RIDE India, Childline etc. have been working to eradicate child labour in India. Child labour has also been a subject of public interest litigations in many Indian courts.

Abolition of child trafficking, elimination of poverty, free and compulsory education, and basic standards of living can reduce the problem to a great extent. The World Bank and International Monetary Fund can help in eradicating poverty by providing loan to the developing countries.

Strict implementation of labour laws is also essential in order to prevent exploitation by parties or multinational companies. Many amendments are required in the present child labour prohibition law in order to implement strict measures to control the situation. The minimum age of fourteen years needs to be increased to at least eighteen. By allowing children below the age of 14 years to work in non-hazardous industries we are only encouraging child labour and not abolishing it. This implies that our legislature has not prescribed a minimum age for child labour. All persons below the age of 18 are considered to be a child by our Constitution, then why are there demarcations in the Child Labour Law? The list of hazardous activities which are present in the law needs to include more occupations which have been left out of the purview of the hazardous activities. More than anything else, normal and healthy childhood is the right of every child and it should not be taken away from them in the name of poverty, adverse conditions of the family or even for that matter, in the name of technicalities of the law.

12

Customary and Reflective Morality

Ethics also known as moral philosophy, is a branch of philosophy that involves systematizing defending, and recommending concepts of right and wrong conduct. The terms comes from the Greek word ethics, which means "Character". Ethics is a complement to aesthetics in the philosophy field of axiology. In Philosophy, ethics studies the moral behaviour in human and how one should act. It answer the question "What do I do?" At a more fundamental level, it is the method by which we categorise our values and pursue them. Do we pursue our own happiness, or do we sacrifice ourselves to a greater cause? Is that foundation of ethics based on the Bible, or on the very nature of man himself, or neither? Should we use principle or rules or laws, or should we let each situation decide our morality? Are killing lying cheating, stealing, and sexual acts right or wrong and why or why not? Ethics, them, seems to pertain to the individual character of a person or person. In philosophy, the term ethics is also used to refer a specific area of study.

Scope

Ethics may be divided into four major area of study:

- Psychological about the theoretical meaning and reference of moral propositions and how their truth values (if any) may be determined;
- Social about the practical means determining a moral course of action;
- The theory of ethical standard about how moral outcomes can be achieved in specific situations;

- Practical also known as comparative ethics, is the study of peoples beliefs about morality.

The point, is that a complete study of ethics demands use of the descriptive, the normative, and the meta-ethical approaches. It is a important for ethicists to draw on any and all data and on valid results of experiments from the naturally physical, and social science. They also examine their language, logic and foundations. But it seems even more crucial for ethicists to contribute something towards helping all human beings to live with each other more meaningfully and more ethically. If philosophy cannot contribute to this latter imperative, then human ethics will either be decide haphazardly by each individual for himself or by unexamined religious pronouncements. My own commitment, then is to a synthesis of descriptive, normative and analytic ethics, with heavy emphasis on putting ethics to use in the human community, which means a heavier emphasis on the normative.

Nature

Ethics is a requirement for human life. It is our means of deciding a course of action. Without it our actions would be random and aimless even with an ethical standard we may unable to pursue our goals with the possibility of success. To the degree which a rational ethical standard is taken, we are able to correctly organise our goals and actions to accomplish our most important values. Any flaw in our ethics will reduces our ability to be successful in our endeavours.

A proper foundation of ethics requires a standard of value to which all goals and actions can be compared to. This standard of value, the goal in which an ethical man must always aim. It is arrived at by an examination of man's nature, and recognising his peculiar needs. A system of ethics must further consist of not only emergency situations, but the day-to-day choices we make constantly. It must include our relations to others, and recognise their importance not only others, and recognise their importance not only to our physical survival, but to our well-being and happiness. It must recognise that our lives are an end in themselves, land that sacrifice is not only not necessary, but destructive.

Ethics is a normative science. It is concerned with what ought to be done rather than what is the case. It differs from positive science. A positive natural science or descriptive science is concerned with what is. Ethics does not deal with facts. Rather it deals with values. Therefore, it is clear that ethics is concerned with judgment of values. Normative ethics deals with standards or norms by which we can judge human actions to be right or wrong.

A norm or ideal in the ethical sense is defined as any regulatory principle that controls or lays guidelines to thought and mode of acting. Ethics is a science of values as it discovers the forms on conduct or behaviour, which have the character of oughtness. Ethics deals with moral phenomena and it observes and classifies them and explains them by the moral ideal. It distinguishes moral judgment from logical judgments and aesthetic judgment and reduce them to a system. So, we may define the nature of ethics as scientific. However, from another perspective all science also lead to philosophical questions if we take philosophy to be quest for knowledge that is why ethics is a branch of philosophy.

What is Morality?

In common parlance, morality is directly related to the conduct of an individual. Morality comes from the Latin word *Moralis*, meaning customs or manners. The study of morality pertains to questions like what is good, bad, right or wrong in a moral sense.

It is interesting to note that Aristotle (384–322 B.C.) argued that being moral had to do with the function of a human being. And that in developing his argument he moved from the non-moral to the moral uses of "good" and "bad". He suggested that anything that was good or bad was so because it functioned well or poorly. He then went on to say that if we could discover what the function of human beings is, then we would know how the terms good or bad could be applied to humans. Having arrived at the theory that the proper function of human beings was to reason, he concluded that being moral was therefore reasoning well for a complete life.

Customary or Traditional Morality

We are all born into customary or traditional morality: it is the first morality that exists in various cultures and societies is usually based on custom or tradition, and it is presented to its members, often without critical analysis or evaluation, throughout their childhood and adult years. There is nothing necessarily wrong or bad about this approach to training the young of a society and also its members as a whole. Many moral teachings have arisen out of human need in social interaction and have become customs and traditions in a particular society. For example, in peace, one of the first moral teachings or one of the first moral teachings or rules has to be about taking human life because, obviously, if life is constantly in danger, then it is very difficult for people to live and work together. However, in order for customs and traditions to be effective and continuously applicable to the members of a society, they must be critically analysed, tested, and evaluated and this is where reflective morality comes in.

Reflective Morality: Philosophers urge human beings to use reason to examine the basis and effectiveness of all moral teaching or rules, no matter how traditional or accepted they are. In other words philosophy requires human beings to reflect on their moral customs and traditions to determine whether they should be retained or eliminated. The great Greek philosopher Socrates (4702-399 B.C.) said, "The unexamined life is not worth living." For morality, a corollary might be, the unexamined custom or tradition is not worth living by. Therefore, just as people should not accept statements or propositions for which there is no proof for significant logical argument so they should not accept moral customs or traditions without first testing them against proof, reason, and their experience.

A good example of reflective morality is an examination of the aforementioned Ten Commandments, which many people in Western culture swear by and claim to follow Interestingly enough, a good many people don't even know what most of them are, with the possible exception of the one against commuting adultery, which everyone seems to know and often cannot even list them in order or otherwise. Further, how many have examined them as I have suggested earlier and realised that they apply to different aspects of morality? How many people realise that the first three commandments apply only to human beings in relationship to a supernatural being or beings, that commandments four through eight apply to their relationships with others whereas nine and ten basically apply to themselves as individuals.

It is important, then, that all customs, traditions, system of ethics, rules, and ethical theories be carefully analysed and critically evaluated before we continue to accept or live by them. Again, we should not reject them out of hand, but neither should we endorse them wholeheartedly unless we have subjected them to careful, logical sauternes.

Distinction between Customary and Reflective Morality

The intellectual distinction between customary and reflective morality is clearly marked. The former places the standard and rules of conduct in ancestral habit; the latter appeals to conscience reason or to some principle which includes thought. The distinction is as important as it is definite, for it shifts the centre of gravity in morality. Nevertheless the distinction is reflective thought must have entered occasionally into systems which in the main were founded on social wont and use, while in contemporary morals, even when the need of critical judgment is most recognition, there is an immense amount of conduct that is merely accommodated to social usage. In what follows we shall accordingly, emphasise the difference in principle a revolution was wrought when Hebrew prophets and Greek seers asserted that conduct is not truly conduct unless it springs from the heart, from personal desires and affections, or from personal insight and rational choice. The change was revolutionary not only because it displaced custom from the supreme position but even more because it entailed the necessity of criticising existing customs and institutions from a new point of view. Standards which were regarded by the followers of tradition as the basis of duty and responsibility were denounced by prophet and philosopher as the source of moral corruption. These proclaimed the hollowness of outer conformity and insisted upon the cleansing of the heart and the clarifying of the mind as preconditions of any genuinely good conduct.

For instance, we should respect our elders is a customary moral. But asking that why should we are so or should we respect them in all circumstances, is a reflective moral.

Customary morality surely unproblematic but then reflective morality is the need of the hour. It does not mean that we should put away our customs or traditions, just that we should rationalise them and then decide whether we want to accept them or not. Reflective morality is pragmatic in nature.

13

Kant's Notion of Categorical Imperatives

Kantian ethics is a form of deontological ethics – an ethical theory that defines right independently of the good. Some theories are teleological: that is, they define right by reference to the good – usually, the good that the action produces. Kant seems to deny any consequentialist element to his theory. Instead, whether or not it conforms to what he terms the moral law, the categorical imperative. Our duties can be understood in terms of respecting this imperative, even if respecting the moral law leads to bad effects rather than good ones. For example, we are obligated to keep our promises, even when keeping them result in less good. One of the ideas underlying Kant's approach is that what makes an action wrong, then, is not the bad it produces, but something else, the kind of action that it is.

Kant believed that morality was prior. He believed that in investigation morals we need to look at pure practical reason. Morality would hold not just for beings with our nature, but for all rational beings. The moral law, them, must be sought a prior, independent of the peculiarities of our nature. He writes in the *Grounding for the metaphysics of morals*: the ground of obligation here must therefore be sought not in the nature of man nor in the circumstances of the world in which man is placed, but must be sought a priori solely in the concepts of pure reason.

His emphasis on autonomy and his anti-consequentialism have, for example, informed a good deal of policy that has been implemented in medical ethics surrounding patients rights. It follows from Kant's view that lying to patients even for the sake of their own good is impermissible misleading patients about therapies and experimental procedures again for the sake of the good, is impermissible and so forth. A good will is good not because of what it performs or effects not by its aptness for the attainment of some proposed end, but simply by virtue of the volition, that is it is good in itself, and considered by itself is to be esteemed much higher than all that can be brought about by it in favour of any inclination, many, even of the sum-total of all inclinations. The emphasis that he placed on respect for autonomy, as opposed to mere concern for well-being or happiness can be seen in policies that make clear that the individual has the right to be treated with respect and not simply benevolence.

Genuine moral duties are categorical and unconditional. The source of moral authority is not to be found in human nature at all. For example, if moral duty is unconditional duty, then its authority is not contingent on features of our nature such as our emotions, which can be fickle and unreliable. Rather, the ground of morality is found in pure reason. Animals, for example, lacking reason, are neither around by nor covered by moral norms of duty or obligation.

Categorical vs. Hypothetical Imperatives

The moral law is categorical rather than hypothetical and it is an imperative.

Imperatives are commands or orders. A hypothetical imperative is a contingent command, one that we ought to follow given our desires, for example, "Go to the doctor" is a good command to need if we want to get well. That would be an example of a hypothetical imperatives. A categorical imperatives alone have the purport of a practical law and not just the will, however binds us no matter what our desires are "Don't just use someone for your own purposes is obligatory even if we actually have a desire, or want to manipulate someone else. We ought to tell the truth, even if it is unwelcome and so on. This is the nature of morality obligation binds independent of our desires; they are not based in desire but in reason.

Duty vs. Inclination

Kant believed, that when we act well and are solely motivated by good inclination our actions lack moral worth. Animals after all, act on inclination. What differentiates us from them is our capacity to use reason, to make rational judgments about what we ought to do. A person can exhibit moral worth while still experiencing psychological conflict. In a famous passage Kant writes about a person whose mind is:

> ...clouded over with his own sorrow so that all sympathy with the lot of others is extinguished, and suppose him still to have the power to benefit others in distress, even though he is not touched by their trouble because he is sufficiently absorbed with his own: and now suppose that, even though no inclination moves him any longer, he nevertheless tears himself from his deadly insensibility and performs the action without any inclination at all but solely from duty- then for the first time his action has genuine moral worth.

What is important to moral worth is whether or not the sense of duty is what is motivation our action. Inclination can be there too, but need not be. Kant believed that our inclinations are basically just desires that we have punishing us in a certain direction. These desires are too fickle a basis to provide firm moral motivation. The content of our desires changes, but the commands of reason do not.

If a person acts rightly because of duty and not simply because he desires the good, or had an inclination to seek it, them: .... For the first time does his conduct have real moral worth. Undoubtedly in this way also are to be understood those passages of scripture which command us to love our neighbourhood and even our enemy. For love as an inclination cannot be commanded: but beneficence from duty, when no inclination impels us and even when a natural and unconquerable aversion opposes such beneficence, is practical and not pathological love. Such love resides in the will and not in the propensities of feeling. In principles of action and not in tender sympathy: and only this practical love can be commanded.

This degree of psychological hygiene will strike many as rather cold. Critics of Kant will argue that in this respect they demotes some of our most significant emotions-who wants to be loves as a matter of duty?

Marcia Bason, defend the Kantian outlook. He argues that stocker has spelled out the case in a away that does not accurately represent how Kant would approach this issue.

To be fair to Kant, however, we should be quite clear that he is not saying that these "positive emotions are in any way bad. Emotions such as pathological love can be very good indeed but they have no moral worth. We can value them, even if we are not justified in respecting or esteeming them. So, when someone, for example, overcomes temptation by force of a good will, that is worthy of respect, a special kind of valuing. We more than like good wills, we respect them. On this view, it may make sense to encourage and praise actions that happened to correspond to the dutiful, but such action is not worthy of moral admiration.

The Categorical Imperative

Given that moral worth consists in following the moral law, the categorical imperative, what is it? How exactly do we follow it?

Formulation One

Kant's first formulation of the categorical imperative is as follows:

Act only according to that maxim whereby you can at the same time will that it should become a universal law.

Kant argued that in thinking about whether or not to perform an action, we are to first formulate a maxim describing the action, we then test the maxim against the categorical imperative.

Kant goes over a variety of examples to illustrate how this is supposed to work. We will take the case of a man who needs to borrow money, though he knows he cannot repay it. He wants to promise to repay, even though he knows he cannot. Is this morally permissible? Well, first we need to describe the prospective action from the point of view of the agent; that is, the agent, is trying to determine what to do, needs to first formulate a maxim describing the action in question. In this case, the maxim would look something like this, "when I believe myself to be in need of money, I will borrow money and promise to pay it back, although I know that I can never do so."

In testing this against the first formulation of the categorical imperative, we then ask, what if this were a universal law? According to Kant, it is clear that this cannot be universalised. We would get a contradiction in conception. The standard interpretations, attributed to H.J. Paton, holds that Kant means that we cannot will the universality of lying promises, since this would be self-contradictory. That is we would actually get a logical contradiction.

So, we cannot will this to be universal because we cannot even conceive of a world in which everyone makes lying promises successfully universal lying would undermine trust in communication.

There is also a practical contradiction in the lying promise case. The maximum would be something like "I will make a false promise to get a foam I want". When this is universalised, however, people wouldn't be able to get loans because no one would lend them money it they couldn't rely on the promises thus, the frustration of the agents purposes and therein lies the practical contradiction.

We have discussed two interpretations of the first way we can get a contradiction the contraction in conception.

The universalisation test can produce another kind of contradiction, too contradiction in the will or autonomy of the will. The classic case is that of benevolence. Suppose that Robert is considering a donation to charity but is very reluctant, because he would rather spend the money on a new stereo, so he considers a maxim "I will not give anything to charity. This is not universal because if Robert is rational he will realise that he would not want to live in a world in which no one gave to charity. Further Robert should realise that he might, himself, come to need the benevolence of others and then would certainly want there to be some charity in the world."

Exercise of the will requires the capacity for autonomous decision-making and it also requires having our basic needs met in order to be autonomous agents. Thus, in the benevolence case we could not will that failures of benevolence be universalised, since that would be like willing a world in which these conditions were not met.

Formulation Two

The second formulation is:

Act in such a way that you treat humanity, whether in your own person or in the person of another always at the same time as an end and never simply as a means.

Kant is not saying that we can never use another person as a means to our own ends; he is not saying that it is always wrong to do so. When Melissa goes grocery shopping, she uses the store clerks as means to get her groceries. This is fine, as long as she is not treating them simply, or merely as means as long as she is treating them with respect. This entails a respect for them as autonomous rational, beings. If the store clerks are working voluntarily, they are freely consenting to be store clerks, then Melissa does not violate their autonomy when she uses them to do things such as checking out her purchases, loading up her cart, and so forth. Rational nature exists as an end in itself.

How does this apply to some of Kant's own case? Again, consider the lying promise example. If Ann were to fie to Bob, she would be using Bob merely as a means to her own end. This is in clear violation of the categorical imperative.

The duty to tell the truth is perfect. The duty to beneficence is imperfect.

Conclusion

Kant's view has often been associated with a kind of absolutism about rights.

There are many modern ethicists who have been influenced by Kant's ethical, theory, though they reject some of his actual prescriptions. For example, many would argue that his absolutism about duty is too severe. They believe that ethics is duty base, not a function of what consequences are produced by a given action. They might, for example, believe, that there is a hierarchy of duties, and the possibility that duties can sometimes conflict. Consider the lying case again. We do have a duty to tell the truth, but we could also hold that we have a duty to save innocent life when feasible, and in case in which there is a conflict between the two in which we need toile to save the innocent life then we should go with the weightier, that of saving the innocent life. The challenge to the duty-based approach is to soften absolutism without seeming to reduces itself to just another form of consequentialism.

Kant simply wanted to give emotion a subordinate role, not eliminate it altogether. He felt that morality could not be based upon emotion: otherwise it would lose its authority over our actions. Emotions, unlike reason, are fickle and transitory. They resist the pull of reason.

References: Some parts of this chapter have been taken from *The Categorical Imperative: A Study in Kant's Moral Philosophy* Paperback – October 1, 1971 by H.J. Paton and *"Immanuel Kant: The Duties of the Categorical Imperative", section 2.3 from the book Business Ethics (v. 1.0)* and from lectures delivered at Hindu College, University of Delhi.

14

Capital Punishment

Capital punishment is one of the consequences of treating a juvenile as an adult. It is therefore, imperative to analyse the very concept of capital punishment and the consequences which entail from it.

There is an ancient tradition, going back to biblical times but endorsed by the mainstream of philosophers from Plato to Thomas Aquinas, from Hobbes to Kant, Thomas Jefferson, John Stuart Mill and C.S. Lewis that a fitting punishment for murder is the execution of the murderer. One prong of this tradition the backward-looking or deontological position, epitomised in Aquinas and Kant, hold that because human beings as rational agents, have dignity, one who with malice aforethought kills a human being, forfeits his or her right to life and deserves to die. The other forward-looking or consequentiality tradition, exemplified by Jeremy Bentham, Mill and Ernest Van den Haag, holds that punishment ought to serve as a deterrent and that capital punishment is an adequate deterrent to prospective murderers.

Abolitionists such as Hugo Adam Bedau and Jeffrey Reiman deny both prongs of the traditional case for the death penalty. They hold that long prison sentence are a sufficient retributive response to murder and that the death penalty probably does not serve as a deterrent.

Louis P. Pojman holds a combined theory of punishment: a backward-looking judgment that the criminal has committed a heinous crime plus a forward-looking judgment that a harsh punishment will deter would be murderers are sufficient to justify the death penalty.

Louis P. Pojman has given the following arguments in favour of the Death Penalty:

(1) Retribution

Human beings have dignity as self-conscious rational agents who are able to act morally. One could maintain that it is precisely, their moral goodness or innocence that bestows dignity and a right to life on them. Intentionally taking the life of an innocent human being is so evil that the perpetrator forfeits his own right to life. He or she deserves to die.

The retributivist holds three propositions: (i) that all the guilty deserve to be punished; (ii) that only the guilty deserve to be punished; and (iii) that the guilty deserve to be punished in proportion to the severity of their crime.

People often confuse retribution with revenge. While moral people will feel outrage at acts of heinous crimes, such as those described above by Royko, the moral justification of punishment is not vengeance but desert. Vengeance signifies inflicting harm on the offender out of anger because of what he has done. Retribution is the rationally supported theory that the criminal deserves a punishment fitting to the gravity of his crime. Retributivism is the theory that the criminal deserves to be punished and deserves to be punished in proportion to the gravity of his or her crime-weather or not the victim or anyone else desires it. We may all deeply regret having to carry out the punishment, but consider it warranted. When a society fails to punish criminals in a way thought to be proportionate to the gravity of the crime, the danger arises that the publish would take the law into its own hands, resulting in vigilante justice lynch mobs and private acts of retribution. The outcome is likely to be an anarchist, insecure state of injustice. As such, legal retributions stands as a safeguard for an orderly application of punitive desert.

(2) Deterrence

The second tradition justifying the death penalty is the forward-looking utilitarian theory of deterrence. This holds that by executing conflicted murderers we will deter would be murderers from killing innocent people. A common-sense case can be made for deterrence.

The general common-sense argument goes like this:

(i) What people fear more will have a greater deterrence effect on them.

(ii) People fear death more than they do any other human punishment.

(iii) Therefore, people will be deterred more by the death penalty, than by any other humane punishment.

One thing, as Wilson and Herrnstein have argued, a great deal of crime is committed on a cost-benefit schema, wherein the criminal engages in some form of risk assessment as to his or her chances of getting caught and punished in some manner. If her or she estimates the punishment to be mild, the crime becomes inversely attractive and vice-versa. The fact that those who are condemned to death generally do everything in their power to get their sentences postponed or reduced to long-term prison sentences, in the way lifers do not shows that they fear death more than life in prison.

John Stuart Mill admitted that capital punishment does not inspire terror in hardened criminals but it may well make an impression on prospective murderers.

It is noteworthy that prominent abolitionists, such as Charles Black, Hugo Adam Bedau, Ramsey Clark and Henry Schwartzchild have admitted to Ernest Van Den Haag that even if every execution were to deter 100 murders they would oppose it, from which Van Den Haag concludes: "to these abolitionist leaders, the life of every murderer is more valuable than the lives of a hundred prospective victims, for these abolitionists would spare the murderer, even if doing so will cost a hundred future victims their lives."

The death penalty reminds us that there are consequences to our actions and that we are responsible for what we do, so that dire consequences for immoral actions are eminently appropriate. The death penalty is such a fitting response to evil.

Stephen Nathanson has given arguments against capital punishment. He says we can assume that all who support the death penalty and whose views we take seriously are committed to the values of justice and respect for human life. His goal is to show that the death penalty is inconsistent with these values.

If a punishment deters more murders and thus saves more innocent lives, then it is justifiable. While this sounds plausible, it is false and thus fails to justify the death penalty. Nathanson offers two arguments to show this.

First, we can imagine punishments that have greater deterrent value than either the death penalty or imprisonment and yet would be wrong to inflict. Suppose we could deter more murderers by executing not just the person who commits a murder but also the family or closest friends of such a person. If, as it is often said the death penalty is supposed to make potential murderers "think twice" this punishment would be likely to make them think three or four times. Its logic is the same as the argument used to support the death penalty over long-term imprisonment. Yet even if this punishment succeeded, it would be an unjust, immoral punishment. It would save some innocent people's lives by killing other innocent people and this is morally unacceptable. It shows that a punishment can be the best deterrent and still be morally wrong.

Many people support the death penalty for a different reason. They think it is the only truly just punishment for murder and they often feel that anything less than death is morally unacceptable. In explaining this view, many people cite the expression "an eye for an eye."

There are three serious problems for "an eye for an eye." First, it requires unjust and barbaric punishments in cases where people have acted barbarically. Second, it conflicts with many of our beliefs about punishment and its justification. Third, in many cases, it provides no real guidance in determining the appropriate punishments.

Kant acknowledges that the " eye for an eye" principle cannot be applied to all cases and that it sometimes recommends punishments that would be immoral to inflict. Kant believes that raping the rapist, forcing the pederast to have homosexual sex, or forcing the guilty of bestiality to have sex with animals would be "crimes against humanity." Instead, he proposes castration for the rapist and exile for the person guilty of sex with animals. Whatever its customary force and initial plausibility the "eye for an eye" principle is far from the last word on the appropriate punishment for particular crimes and cannot bear the burden of justifying death as a punishment for murder.

Nathanson says suppose that the death penalty deters more effectively than other punishments and suppose that murderers deserve to die. In addition, however, suppose that the legal institutions of a society that imposes the death penalty are not reliable. As a result innocent people are often convicted of murder. Suppose, for example, that half of those convicted were innocent and that people know about the failings of the system. In this situation, even though the death penalty is justified in theory, it would be unjustified in practice.

Nathanson's claim is that if death penalty supporters consider their own values, they will see that these values are violated by the institution of capital punishment both as it exists now and as it is almost certain to exist for the foreseeable future.

Since there is widespread view that only some of those people who kill others deserve to die, a just system must be capable of two things : first, it must separate the guilty from the innocent and, second, it must be able to sort out the worst murderers. If the system cannot do both of these reliably, then the results that it generates are unjust. In theory, the death penalty is imposed because of the terribleness of the specific crimes committed. In practice, actual death sentences are the result of arbitrary, irrelevant factors like race, socio-economic status and the quality of legal representation. Anyone concerned with the value of human life would be determined to insure that executions occur only after the most exacting procedures have proved beyond a reasonable doubt that death is the proper punishment. There is an obvious inconsistency between affirming the value of human life and tolerating the current level of legal representation for people who face the possibility of death. Problems with our system can lead to two kinds of mistaken judgment. The first is that a person who is guilty of a crime may receive a more severe punishment than would have been received had he or she been a member of a different race, had a higher social status or had been able to hire a better lawyer. The second is that the poor quality of legal representation may result in innocent people being convicted of murder and sentenced to die.

We know that death sentences will result from racial prejudice, poor legal representation and misdeeds by police and prosecutors. We know that evidence of innocence will be rejected by courts because deadlines are missed. We know that the practice of capital punishment as it actually exists violates the principles of justice and respect for human life. Anyone who genuinely cares about justice and the value of human life should conclude that the death penalty should be put to reset.

15

Is Age Just a Number? A Perspective on Juvenile Justice System in India

In late 1970s, the Pulitzer Prize winning historian Barbara Tuchman declared: "Of all the characteristics in which the medieval age differs from the modern, none is so striking as the comparative absence of interest in children". So central is the question of child rights in the modern world that the presence of a highly developed Juvenile Justice code has become an imperative for any modern judicial system.

In the modern world, one of the first institutions dedicated to juvenile delinquency was the New York House of Refuge, in 1825 in the United States of America, which focused on moral rehabilitation of delinquent youth. The first juvenile court in the world was also established in the same country in 1899 at the Cook County in the State of Illinois.

India developed its own jurisprudence relating to children and the recognition of their rights with the adoption of the Constitution on the 26th November 1949 it was guaranteed that several rights be extended to children - such as equality before the law, free and compulsory primary education to children between the age group of six to fourteen years, prohibition of trafficking and forced labour of children and prohibition of employment of children below the age of 14 years in factories, mines or hazardous activities.

The Juvenile Justice (Care and Protection) Act, 2000 [JJCPCA], was enacted after years of deliberation and in conformity with international standards as laid down in the United Nations Convention on the Rights of the Child, 1989, the Beijing Rules, 1985, the Havana Rules and other international instruments for securing the best interests of the child with the primary object of social reintegration of child victims and children in conflict with law, without resorting to conventional judicial proceedings which existed for adult criminals.

The JJCPCA, 2000, is in consonance with the provisions of the Constitution and the various Declarations and Conventions adopted by the world community represented by the United Nations. The basis of fixing of the age till when a person could be treated as a child at eighteen years in the JJCPCA, 2000, was Article 1 of the Convention of the Rights of the Child and reducing the age from 18 to 16 years would be against the UN Convention, which India ratified in 1992.

Scientific data indicates that the brain continues to develop and the growth of a child continues till the age of eighteen and it is then that he can be held fully responsible for his actions. Along with physical growth, mental growth is equally important, in assessing the maturity of a person below the age of eighteen years. Competence-related abilities mature by sixteen, but the capacity relevant to decisions about criminal culpability continues to mature till young adulthood. These findings of the MacArthur Foundation, are supported by later brain science researchers such as Laurence Steinberg who argues in his paper "Should the Science of Adolescent Brain Development Inform Public Policy?" (*Issues in Science and Technology*, Spring 2012) thus: "Adolescents should be viewed as inherently less responsible than adults, and should be punished less harshly than adults, even when crimes they are convicted of are identical."

Moreover, a 2011 research based on the United States federal government's 'National Longitudinal Survey of Youth' undertaken by Prof. Robert Brame submitted that "by age 23, almost a third of Americans have been arrested atleast once". More importantly, the researchers found that the probability of a first arrest accelerated in late adolescence and early adulthood — at 18, 15.9 per cent of the participants reported having been arrested — and then began to flatten out as the youths entered their 20s. Thus, the fact that crime rates peak at the age 18 marks the writing on the wall that indeed the juvenile justice laws need to be extended to this upper limit of eighteen. We must remember the age old maxim –

> *"Ad ea quae frequentius acciduuntjuraadaptantur"*

(The laws are adapted to those cases, which occur more frequently)

In conjunction with psychological reasons, there are economic aspects as well which act as determinants in relation to the question of whether the juvenile age should be reduced to sixteen. According to the recent National Crime Records Bureau [NCRB] statistics, 52.9 per cent juveniles apprehended in 2012 belonged to families with annual incomes less than Rs 25,000, this figure went up to 55.6 per cent in 2014. Similarly, 52 per cent juveniles apprehended in 2012 were either illiterate or educated up to primary level, in 2014 the number went up to 53 per cent. So, it can be concluded with a degree of certainty that, majority of the juvenile delinquents come from poor economic backgrounds and hence, there seems to be a truly causal relationship between juvenile crime and poverty. Often, it has been argued by social scientists that one of the most deteriorating impacts of poverty on children is caused due to lack of proper educational facilities and therefore, those juveniles convicted for heinous crimes should be given education instead of punishing them. Perhaps in accordance with the same line of reasoning, Justice KG Balakrishnan said in one of his recent interviews "A village boy of sixteen years, what maturity can we attribute to him? In a well-educated family of fair means, sixteen years may be a good age. But the same cannot be true in the case of ordinary, poor citizens."

It needs to be considered, that if a child is sent to jail, after trial in an ordinary criminal court, there is no likelihood of any reformation and he would come out a hardened criminal owing to harsh conditions and more importantly, the social stigmatisation of the juvenile delinquent as a criminal and social outcaste. This is a social outcome that has been duly emphasised by thinkers and social scientists such as George Herbert Mead, David Matza and more recently Erving Goffman, basing their conclusions on extensive research. Therefore, utmost care must be observed before reducing the age to sixteen years.

The Juvenile Justice Amendment Bill which states that children in the 16-18 age group to be tried as adults if they commit heinous crimes violates the fundamental rights guaranteed under Article 14 and Article 15(3) of the Constitution. Moreover, of the 472 million children of the country, only 1.2 per cent have committed crimes. And that, of these, only 2.17 per cent had committed murder and 3.5 per cent had committed rape and amidst the ambiguity embedded in the definitions of the proposed law, it would be preposterous to put a large number of the remaining innocent juveniles at risk. In fact, it needs to be recognised, as has been pointed out by a long line of sociologists such as Robert Merton, Sutherland and Robert Agnew that the cause of juvenile delinquency is often the failure of the social structure to accommodate people from diverse socio-economic backgrounds in its fold. It is therefore, no surprise that the U.S. Supreme Court, in *Stanford v. Kentucky*[24], strongly endorsed the observation of the Task Force on Sentencing Policy Towards Young Offenders thus : "Youth crime... is not exclusively the offender's fault; offences by the young represent a failure of family, school and social system, which share responsibility for the (ir) development..."

A law should be just in nature. It should never be passed in haste and out of angst. The juvenile age had been fixed at eighteen after due deliberation and on obtaining much scientific evidence in its support and hence, it should not be reduced to sixteen years just because the public is angry with the release of the Nirbhaya case juvenile delinquent. Especially in formulation of laws, as they say, *Abundans Cautela Non Nocet* (abundant caution does no harm) since history is testimony to the fact that reactive laws formulated in haste, as a result of a knee-jerk reaction of the society are often incohate and thereby, prove to be unsustainable for the very society that demands it.

16

What According to Aristotle is the Highest Moral Ideal?

Knowledge, according to Aristotle, is of three main kinds- theoretical, practical or productive, according as it is pursued for its own sake, as a means to conduct, or as a means to making something that is useful or beautiful. The supreme practical science- that to which all others are subordinate and ministerial is politics. Of this science ethics is just a part and accordingly Aristotle never speaks of 'ethics' as a separate science but only of 'the study of character' or 'our discussions of character.'

Aristotle's ethics, no doubt, are social and his politics are ethical; he does not forget in the Ethics that the individual man is essentially a member of society, nor in the politics that the good life of the state exists only in the good lives of its citizens.

At the outset of the Ethics he describes the good of the state as greater and more perfect than that of the individual and the latter as merely something with which we may have to put up if we cannot attain the former. But his sense of the value of the individual life appears to grow as he discusses it and at the end of the work he speaks as if the state were merely ancillary to the moral life of the individual, supplying the element of compulsion which is needed if man's desires are to be made subservient to his reason.

The keynote of the Ethics is struck in the first sentence: 'Every art and every enquiry, every action and choice seems to aim at some good: the good has rightly been defined as that at which all things aim.

Aristotle's ethics is definitely teleological morality because for him good consists in doing certain actions not because we see them to be right in themselves but because we see them to be such as will bring us nearer to the 'good for man'. The end at which a particular action aims may be but a means to a further end but there must be a term to this series each action must have an ultimate end which is valuable in itself and Aristotle infers too readily, the ultimate end of all actions must be the same.

Ethics reasons not from but to first principles; it starts not with what is intelligible in itself but with what is familiar to us, i.e. with the bare facts and works back from them to the underlying reasons; and to give the necessary knowledge of the facts a good upbringing is necessary.

Both ordinary people and persons of trained mind define the good as happiness. Ordinary men identify happiness with something obvious and visible, such as pleasure or wealth or honour- everybody gives a different definition and sometimes the same persons own definition alters: when a man has fallen ill he thinks that happiness is health, if he is poor he thinks it is wealth. To judge by men's mode of living, the mass of mankind think that good and happiness consist in pleasure and consequently are content with a life of mere enjoyment. Four main kinds of life seem to be chosen by men. Most men aim at pleasure but this is an end for slaves or beasts. The better sort aim at honour; this is the object of the political life. But honour depends more on the giver than on the receiver, while the end of life must be something that is our very own. Honour seems to be aimed at as something that assures us of our own virtue and virtue is perhaps more truly the end of the political life. But virtue is compatible with inactivity and with misery and on both these counts is disqualified for being the true end. Some men again pursue wealth but this is a means, not an end. Then there is also the life of contemplation which Aristotle believes to be the highest end.

There are two marks which the good for man must possess. It must be final, something that is chosen always for its own sake, never as a means to anything else. And it must be self-sufficient something which by itself makes life worthy of being chosen. But we have to still ask what happiness is. To answer this question, Aristotle introduces the Platonic notion of work or function. He is at bottom asking what kind of life will give a man most satisfaction, but to answer this he finds it necessary to ask what is the characteristic function of man. The question is borrowed from the arts and in them admits of an easy answer. There is no difficulty in seeing that the function of a flute-player as such is to play the flute or that of an axe is to cut. Aristotle answers the question by considering what it is that only man can do. Growth and reproduction we share with animals and plants, sensation with animals' neither of these can be the characteristic work of man. But in man there is superimposed on these faculties a higher faculty. Within this there is a sub-faculty which understands the plan and one which obey it. Well-being must be the life of this faculty. Secondly, it must be activity in accordance with rational principal not mere potentiality. Thirdly, it must be in accordance with virtue, or if there is more than one virtue with the best and most perfect of them. Fourthly, it must be manifested not merely for short periods but in a complete life.

Virtue is the spring from which good activity flows, pleasure its natural accompaniment and prosperity its normal precondition; though Aristotle is careful to add that fine character may 'shine through' adverse circumstances. Well-being activity in accordance with virtue.

It is not like the faculties of sense which are present, Aristotle assumes full-grown from the start; as we learn to be builders by building or harpers by playing the harp, we become just or temperate by doing just or temperate act. The first rule laid down with regard to these activities is that excess and defect are both to be avoided. As either excess or defect of exercise or of food is bad for the body so if we fear everything we shall become cowardly and if we fear nothing we shall become foolhardy; in neither case will courage be developed in us. And the acts we do when we have acquired the virtue will have the same character of moderation as those from which the virtue is developed. Every expert avoids excess and deficiency and adopts the middle amount-not the exact half of the object he is dealing with but a medium quantity in relation to the person concerned. The implication is that excess and deficiency impair excellence and a middle quantity secures it. It is doubtful, however, whether the doctrine of the mean is the correct way of expressing this sane and true view. In so far as virtue involves a certain intensity of feeling or the spending of a certain amount of money or the like there is some appropriateness in describing it as a mean. But the time the object the manner must also be right and Aristotles' attempt to apply a quantitative notion like the mean to these elements in right action is by no means successful. It is not always the case that the right action is in a mean. Even granting that the instinctive feelings are in the abstract indifferent, there are occasions on which a particular feeling should be entirely suppressed and others on which a particular feeling should be followed to the uttermost. It seems to be an accident, though a very frequent accident, of right action that it should be intermediate between extremes. The theory has value as a recognition of the necessity of introducing system or as Aristotle says symmetry, into the manifold tendencies which exist within us. The mean is opposed to excess and deficiency and therefore there is no mean of an excess or a deficiency of a mean. If one of the two extremes appears to be closer than the other to the middle and to resemble it more, we do not consider it but rather the other one as the opposite of the middle. For instance, rashness seems to be more like courage and nearer to it and cowardice seems more unlike it.

We can only be held responsible for actions we perform voluntarily and not for cases involving physical compulsion or unavoidable ignorance. The best measure of moral judgment is choice, since choices are always made voluntarily by means of rational deliberation. We always choose to aim at some apparent good instead, which is, in fact, a vice. Virtues are said to be concerned with feeling and actions. Their scope is defined sometimes by reference to a type of action, but this is only a matter of convenience a virtue is a tendency control a certain class of feeling and to act rightly in a certain kind of situation. Two special points to be noted in the description of the virtues are—

(1) the light which it throws on the doctrine of the mean, and

(2) the intrusion of non-moral elements, of which the accounts of magnificence self-respect and wittiness afford the best

evidence. Magnificence, for example, turns out to be mainly a matter of aesthetic good taste.

Happiness then we define as the active exercise of the mind in conformity with perfect goodness or virtue.

There are then three kinds of dispositions, two of them vices, one a vice of deficiency, and one of virtue which is a middle state and each of the three dispositions is in a manner opposed to both of the others; the extremes are the opposites of each other and the middle is the opposite of each of the extremes because just as in mathematics a is greater then a-b and less then a+b, similarly middle dispositions of character are excessive as compared with the deficiencies and deficient as compared with excesses. This holds good both of emotions and of actions. A brave man appears rash when compared with a cowards and cowardly when compared with a rash man, and similarly a self-controlled man seems self-indulges in comparison with a man insensitive to pleasure and pain but insentient in comparison with a self-indulgent one. Although the two extreme dispositions are opposed in this way to the middle one, it is the two extremes that are most widely opposed, as these are further away from each other than they are from the middle.

A small departure from the right amount, either in the direction of excess or of deficiency, is not censured, though a wider divergence is bound to be noticed. The questions of degree depend on the particular circumstances, and can only be judged by intuition. This much then is clear, that the middle course in everything is commendable, but that we should diverge sometimes towards excess and sometimes towards deficiency, as that is the easiest way of hitting the middle course, which is the right one.

If Aristotle's ethics is practiced in day-to-day life it would help one in understanding the theory of reforming juvenile offenders. Moreover, it would provide us with better comprehension of child psychology, which would in turn help in dealing with them and formulating as well as executing child legislations and rights.

References: Some parts of this chapter have been taken from S.F. (2002). Sarah Broadie and Christopher Rowe (Eds) *Aristotle*

Nicomachean Ethics: Translation, Introduction, and Commentary. (Oxford: Oxford University Press, 2002), *Religious Studies* 38 (3): 371-37, Aristotle (2004) *The Nichomachean Ethics*, Penguin Books and from lectures delivered at Hindu College, University of Delhi.

Bibliography

1. The National Commission for Women: A Study In Performance, by Sadhna Arya, pp. 1-3.
2. 1967 AIR 1643.
3. AIR 1973 SC 1461.
4. International Men and Gender Equality Survey (IMAGES).
5. "India tackles domestic violence". BBC News, 2006-10-27.
6. Sudha G Tilak (2013-03-11), "Crimes against women increase in India."
7. Government of India (2006).
8. B Nagi, Child Marriage in India: A Study of its Differential Patterns in Rajasthan.
9. Child marriage and poverty ICRW, Targeting Girls in the Name of Tradition: Child Marriage, Melanne Verveer (2010).
10. "Combating Acid Violence in Bangladesh, India and Cambodia". Avon Foundation for Women, pp. 1-64 (2011).
11. Sexual Violence Against Women, Vandana.
12. 'Sexual Harassment: The Link Between Gender Stratification, Sexuality and Women's Economic Status' in Women, JO Freeman (ed), 1984, p. 54).
13. Laura J Evan, 'Sexual Harassment: Women's Hidden Occupational Hazard' in The Victimisation of Women, Margaret Gates (ed), 1985, p. 221.
14. Linda Wirth, 'Sexual Harassment at Work' in Promoting Gender Equality at Work-Turning Vision into Reality, 1997, p. 131.
15. AIR 1997 SC 3011.

16. (2013) 1 SCC 311.
17. 68 (1997) DLT 303.
18. 524 U.S. 742 (1998).
19. 524 U.S. 775 (1998).
20. Article: Two concepts of Liberty, Sir Isaiah Berlin.
21. "Child Marriage Facts and Figures" International Center for Research on Women.
22. Literacy Rate Up, But so is Illiteracy; Chethan Kumar | TNN | Jan 28, 2016, 04.01 AM IST.
23. AIR 2003 SC 355.
24. A Blurry Vision: Reconsidering the Failure of the One Laptop Per Child Initiative **Namank Shah** (WR 150, Paper 3).
25. M.P. Jain, Indian Constitution Law (5th ed., 2003).
26. H.M. Seervai, Constitutional Law [4th ed., Vol. 1 (1991), Vol. 2 (1993), Vol. 3 (1996)].
27. *Studies in Jurisprudence and Legal Theories,* 7th edition, by N.V. Paranjape.
28. The Juvenile Justice System in India: From Welfare to Rights, Ved Kumari, 2nd Edition.
29. Human Rights International Challenges, Volume 1 and 2, S. Subramaniam.
30. The Constitution of India, 1950.
31. The Factories Act of 1948.
32. The Mines Act of 1952.
33. The Child Labour (Prohibition and Regulation) Act of 1986.
34. The Juvenile Justice (Care and Protection) of Children Act of 2000.
35. The Right of Children to Free and Compulsory Education Act of 2009.
36. *Criminal Law Amendment Act, 2013.*

37. The Sexual Harassment of Women at Workplace (Prevention, Prohibition and Redressal) Act, 2013.
38. *Dowry Prohibition Act, 1961.*
39. Protection of Women from Domestic Violence Act, 2005.
40. *United Nations Convention on the Rights of the Child (UNCRC), 1989.*
41. Convention on the Elimination of all forms of Discrimination Against Women (CEDAW).
42. Equality Act, 2010.
43. *Pre Natal Diagnostic Techniques Act, 1994.*
44. *The Prohibition of Child Marriage Act, 2006.*
45. Professor Daya Krishan's book, Social Philosophy: Past and Future Published in 1969.
46. Grint 1991: 7.
47. The Categorical Imperative: A Study in Kant's Moral Philosophy Paperback – October 1, 1971 by H. J. Paton.
48. "Immanuel Kant: The Duties of the Categorical Imperative", section 2.3 from the book Business Ethics (v. 1.0).
49. S. F. (2002), Sarah Broadie and Christopher Rowe (Eds) Aristotle Nicomachean Ethics: Translation, Introduction, and Commentary. (Oxford: Oxford University Press, 2002) *Religious Studies* 38 (3): 371-37.
50. Aristotle (2004), The Nichomachean Ethics, Penguin Books.
51. Berlin, I. (1958), *"Two Concepts of Liberty." In* Isaiah Berlin (1969) *Four Essays on Liberty.* Oxford: Oxford University Press.

References

1. The National Commission for Women: A Study in Performance, by Sadhna Arya, pp. 1-3.
2. Studies in Jurisprudence and Legal Theory, Dr N.V. Paranjape, 7th Edition.
3. AIR 1967 SC 1643.
4. AIR 1973 SC 1461.
5. Studies in Jurisprudence and Legal Theory, Dr N.V. Paranjape, 7th Edition.
6. International Men and Gender Equality Survey (IMAGES).
7. "India tackles domestic violence". BBC News, 2006-10-27.
8. Sudha G Tilak (2013-03-11). "Crimes against women increase in India".
9. Government of India (2006).
10. B Nagi, Child Marriage in India: A Study of its Differential Patterns in Rajasthan, ISBN.
11. Child marriage and poverty ICRW, Targeting Girls in the Name of Tradition: Child Marriage, Melanne Verveer (2010).
12. "Combating Acid Violence in Bangladesh, India and Cambodia". Avon Foundation for Women, pp. 1-64 (2011).
13. Sexual Violence Against Women, Vandana.
14. AIR 1997 SC 3011.
15. (2013) 1 SCC 311.
16. 68 (1997) DLT 303.
17. 524 U.S. 742 (1998).
18. 524 U.S. 775 (1998).

19. "Child Marriage Facts and Figures" International Center for Research on Women.
20. Literacy Rate Up, But so is Illiteracy; Chethan Kumar | TNN | Jan 28, 2016, 04.01 AM IST.
21. AIR 2003 SC 355.
22. A Blurry Vision: Reconsidering the Failure of the One Laptop Per Child Initiative Namank Shah (WR 150, Paper 3).
23. Grint 1991: 7.
24. 192 U.S. 361 AT 395-96 (1989).

Index

D

Q

R

S

T